How Far Is Heaven?

How Far Is Heaven?

Rediscovering the Kingdom of God
in the Here and Now

Ronnie McBrayer

WIPF & STOCK · Eugene, Oregon

For Jeffrey and Sue Allen, who quietly change the world,
and who have changed mine.

"If we only had eyes to see and ears to hear and wits to understand, we would know that the Kingdom of God is as close as breathing and it is crying out to be born both within ourselves and within the world.... The Kingdom of God is where we belong. It is home, and whether we realize it or not, I think we are all homesick for it."

—FREDERICK BUECHNER

Contents

Introduction ix

Chapter One The Kudzu Conspiracy / 1

Chapter Two Do No Harm / 9

Chapter Three The Pearl of the World / 18

Chapter Four "The Little Way" / 28

Chapter Five Put Out the Fire / 38

Chapter Six Bleeding Charity / 49

Chapter Seven Where Nothing Is Sacred / 58

Chapter Eight For the Long Haul / 68

Chapter Nine (Un)Doing Justice / 77

Chapter Ten "Go to Jesus!" / 88

Conclusion / 99
Endnotes / 103
Bibliography / 105

Introduction

Jesus went to Galilee preaching the Message of God: "Time's up! God's kingdom is here. Change your life and believe the Message."

—MARK 1:15 (THE MESSAGE)

MORRIS THE BAKER WAS born, married, and had always lived in the same little town. He awoke to his all-too-familiar surroundings early one morning more tired than when he went to bed, feeling bored and disgusted with his life. He looked over at his sleeping wife and asked himself, "Why her?" wondering how he ever ended up with such a woman. Rising from bed and dressing quietly in the dark, he slipped down the hallway and peeped into his children's bedroom. "Why them?" he muttered and walked out of the house. Looking back at his old tumbledown home from the walkway he was overcome with gloom once again. "Why that?" he asked the heavens, and slammed the loose and creaky gate on its hinges.

As Morris walked to the village in the cold morning his mood grew darker still: "I'll never have the money to fix up that old house. My wife never gives me a moment's peace, always angry at me. My children are selfish and too loud with all their nonsense and chatter. I have to slave from morning until night working at the bakery, barely eking out a living." It was then that Morris remembered something his rabbi once said: "Someday we will all go to heaven, a place of peace and plenty, and there everyone is always happy and content and no one will ever know trouble or pain again."

"And how far is heaven?" wondered Morris. "How and when will I, Morris the baker, get to go to heaven?" Suddenly, he answered his own question: "Now!" he cried aloud. "I will go now to find heaven!" So, instead of walking to the bakery in town, Morris started off in the opposite direction (because didn't the old rabbi point in that direction when he talked about heaven?) and off he went toward the far horizon.

He soon came to a mountain and, without a second thought, started up the path to the top. The climb was steep and the sun was hot, but Morris walked all day ignoring his aching feet and the growl in his stomach. "Soon," he thought, "I will be in heaven and have all the food, drink, and rest that I want." As night fell, Morris took off his boots and pointed them in the direction he was walking, so that when he woke up he would know the direction to go and be able to continue his trip to heaven. He then collapsed into a deep sleep.

While the disgruntled baker slept, an angel came along traveling the same path. The angel moved closer and stood over the sleeping Morris, listening to his loud snoring. Then he noticed the boots pointing toward heaven and gave a quiet chuckle. He realized Morris' intentions, and in an act of mischief, turned the boots in the opposite direction and faded into the night, giggling all the way. Morris awoke with the morning sun. He put on his boots and started off in the direction they were pointing.

As he walked, Morris thought he must be getting closer to heaven, because the sun felt so pleasant as he trudged along. Soon the path turned back into an oddly familiar road, and Morris came to an old wooden gate that seemed to be the entrance to heaven. He was surprised it wasn't made of gold or expensive wood. It was creaky and loose on its hinges. Still, he lifted the latch and went into the yard. This yard in heaven looked so much like his yard back home. The door to the wooden house in heaven also looked familiar, just like the door of his earthly house.

The smells of heaven's food made his mouth water and his stomach rumble. He entered the house and sat down at the table in heaven and a woman, so much like his wife, served him a large steaming bowl of soup and a fat roll. The food in heaven was wonderful, and he ate everything put before him. Two young children danced into the kitchen and smiled up at him. These children in heaven were so nice, quiet, and friendly that Morris had to sigh with happiness. "Yes," he thought, "it is exactly as the rabbi said. I have found heaven, and it is simply wonderful."1

This old Yiddish tale is more than a quaint story. It is the truth of the gospel. For when we ask the question, "How far is heaven?" we never have to look beyond the world in which we live. Heaven is right here, right now. Heaven is "under our feet," as Thoreau said, "as well as over our heads."2

This may come as a surprise, but Jesus never described the gospel as an exchange of this current world for a remote spiritual retreat far away. Never. Rather, his gospel was: "God's kingdom is here! It has arrived! It is now! Heaven has come to earth!" So when Jesus invited his disciples—then as well as now—to "Follow me," he was inviting them to get in on the world-redeeming, evil-conquering, status-reversing, life-transforming movement of God that had invaded planet Earth. Jesus, maybe with a clever smile on his face, was pointing our boots back to the place we know best; though, we may have to come to see this place in a whole new light.

"But how can this be?" you may ask. "I thought the gospel was about avoiding hell and going to heaven? Don't we ask Jesus into our hearts so that we can be personally and eternally fulfilled? Isn't this life just a blip on God's eternal screen, a proving ground for the real life to come? Aren't we waiting for Jesus' return when he will flush away this inferior, evil world and replace it with something better?"

No, the good news, as Jesus proclaims it, is not just an evacuation plan to rescue people from earth or the sufferings of the afterlife, transporting them to heaven. Rather, it is a revolutionary strategy to redeem the sufferings of earth by putting the rule and reign of heaven inside of people. Any sharing of the gospel that ignores the needs of this current world, because one's individual status in the next world has been properly secured, is a distortion of the gospel. Any profession of faith that focuses only on enjoying and living in a future heaven, rather than sacrificing for and serving people on today's earth, is not Christian faith. And those who follow a Jesus who concerns himself only with the hereafter, and not bringing holistic change to the here-and-now, are not living out the transforming message of Jesus at all.

In my reading of Jesus' words and actions, I am so certain that he intended to bring the goodness of heaven to today's earth, that even if there were no final heavenly paradise, I would still be a follower of Jesus. Why? Because I believe that the way Jesus taught and empowered us to live is the greatest hope for our world today. Yes, without the promise of a big and final payoff, without the assurance of a celestial reward, without the possibility of pearly gates and streets of gold, I would still have to call myself a Christian. The gospel according to Jesus is that powerful, that ever-present, and that real in this current world.

We discover this fact by taking just a brief look at the Gospels, where Jesus continually stressed the importance of the present kingdom of God (or the equivalent "kingdom of heaven"). It was Jesus' favorite subject by far, dropping from his lips more than a hundred times. While it is a subject that is multifaceted with various applications (we will get to this in the pages ahead), one thing is certain: this kingdom is the redemptive power of God, demonstrated in the person of Jesus, and it is not postponed for a later date. This was made clear as Jesus began his public ministry (see Matthew 4:12–25 and Mark 1:14–38), in his very first recorded sermon (see Luke 4:14–21), in his instruction to the disciples on how they should pray ("Thy kingdom come, thy will be done, on earth as it is in heaven"), and it was affirmed throughout his years of preaching and teaching. But nowhere is this gospel of Jesus made more distinct than in his favorite teaching method: the parables.

At first, Jesus' parables seem harmless—cute and cozy stories for children attending Vacation Bible School. But if we pay closer attention to them, they startle and unsettle us. For you see, by telling stories Jesus wasn't putting sugar in the spoon to make the medicine go down a bit easier. These stories *are* the medicine.3 These stories are an expansion and declaration of Jesus' radical ministry that shatter our tidy, well-packaged ideas about spirituality, faith, and reality. Jesus' parables are sucker-punching, pot-stirring, status quo-bursting tales that pull us in, not to analyze his words, but to participate in his kingdom come to earth. And when we play our part in these stories, something happens which cliché-ridden, cut-and-paste, widgetized spirituality can never accomplish: Jesus begins to change us and, consequently, change the world.4

Of the scores of parables Jesus told, a dozen or so begin with the words, "The kingdom of God is like . . . ." When he said this, he wasn't talking about some far-away, harp-playing, cloud-riding, hymn-singing, glory-praising, pie-in-the-sky heaven. Nor was he talking about mere "social justice"—our human efforts to bring balance to society's books. Jesus did not come to simply reform humanity. He was talking about deliverance, for he came to redeem the lives and souls of people, overcoming all manifestations of evil in this present world. These parables show that urgent, for-this-time-and-place, comprehensive transformation was Jesus' divine mission—thus, this mission also belongs to we who follow him.

This book will explore these parables and encourage us all to reassess the gospel we believe and the role our professed faith plays in the world today (and hopefully turn our boots a bit more toward home). The gospel cannot be used as a type of selfish benefits program, providing us with the privileged comfort of membership, or reduced to apocalyptical escapism whereby we "move on up to that deluxe apartment in the sky." Instead, we must see that the gospel audaciously enters the sorrows of this present world with liberating love, as Jesus can never be locked away "in our hearts." He, his message, and his followers break defiantly free to renew and reshape not only tomorrow, but also the here and now.

The tragedy of missing this message may be best illustrated in the life of my friend Scott, who as a teenager began to experience a stirring deep in his heart that some Christians refer to as "a calling." He had an unmistakable, and absolute divine requisition to service that came from within and without that could not be ignored. So Scott embraced it, attended seminary after college, met and married Karen, and after a few years this couple found themselves working for one of the largest international missions organizations in the world. It was their dream come true. Mexico, Central America, the Middle East, and the Persian Gulf: Scott and Karen traversed the globe for nearly twenty years in faithful service, raising three children, embedding themselves among indigenous people groups and living out the love and witness of Christ.

But it all came to a grinding halt while they were serving in one of the more oppressive Islamic nations of the world, because the organization for which they worked deemed their medical mission financially unsustainable, for reasons other than dollars and cents. Simply, not enough Muslims were becoming Christians.

Conversions.

Baptisms.

Increasing numbers of those praying "the sinner's prayer."

Public professions of faith.

Churches being planted and cross-topped buildings being constructed.

These were the outcomes required by the mission executives, and when these outcomes were not forthcoming, the organization refused to keep pouring millions of dollars into what it officially called an "unreceptive region" of the world.

Scott and Karen pleaded with the mission's executives, who were all safely behind administrative desks in the United States, to reconsider their decision. This was a hostile, dangerous country in which they were serving, a country that required Christians to go "underground," and profess faith quietly and cautiously. Further, the medical facility was serving a huge area of needy people, treating tens of thousands of patients a year. A part of the world that previously hated "western Christianity" was finding it increasingly difficult to hate those who were loving, medicating, and saving their children, sick and elderly.

These appeals were callously ignored. A mission executive responded to the pleas of Scott, Karen, and the medical staff with these words: "We have no obligation to the bodies of those whose souls are going to hell." The facility was defunded, dollars were reallocated to more "productive areas," and the mission's staff, including Scott and Karen, was recalled to the States. To this day, with their hearts largely unhealed, this couple has yet to return to their true calling.

"We have no obligation to the bodies of those whose souls are going to hell."

Is this really the gospel, when we are able to disregard the crushing misery of people today, if those needs are not spiritual in nature? Is it "Good News" when we reduce the love of God to simple statistics, totaling the members sitting in the pews, or counting the numbers who pray a specific, mechanical prayer? Can we, with any integrity, say we are following the way of Jesus if we focus exclusively on the heaven to come while ignoring the heaven "beneath our feet?" The answer to all these questions is an emphatic "No."

Understand, I'm not denying the afterlife, eternal happiness, or a final redemption within a heavenly state—not at all. But I am begging for some much-needed balance as Jesus did not put his emphasis on the hereafter or define the gospel as a form of escapism. Jesus taught, lived, died, and lives again, not so a few select people could earn a seat on a heavenly evacuation pod while everything and everyone else is tossed into the galactic trash can. No, he came to create a community of kingdom-infused people who would make it their vocation—their unmistakable and absolute divine calling that cannot be ignored—to live out God's heaven on earth so that redemption, in all its magnificent and diverse manifestations, will be experienced today, not just tomorrow.

We have the opportunity, if we will take it, to become catalysts and conduits of the very real rule of God here in today's world, because the present—not the future—is where we follow Jesus. Today—not tomorrow—is "the day of salvation" (2 Corinthians 6:2). Here and now—not there and then—is where we live out the blessed hope that is the reign of God. Heaven is not waiting for us on a distant horizon.

It is already well underway.

It is beneath our feet.

It is where we even now call home.

It is the direction our boots are pointing.

It is presently invading earth in and through the practitioners of Jesus' way.

It is breaking free in the world, and that isn't very far away at all.

Chapter 1

The Kudzu Conspiracy

Then Jesus said, "What is the Kingdom of God like? How can I illustrate it? It is like a tiny mustard seed that a man planted in a garden; it grows and becomes a tree, and the birds make nests in its branches." He also asked, "What else is the Kingdom of God like? It is like the yeast a woman used in making bread. Even though she put only a little yeast in three measures of flour, it permeated every part of the dough."

—LUKE 13:18-21 (NLT)

KUDZU ARRIVED IN THE United States as a gift, given by the Japanese as a centennial birthday present, in 1876. It was immediately loved by gardeners, what with its large green leaves and purple blooms, so individuals began planting it and nurseries began selling seedlings through the mail. But it was the Dust Bowl years that really rooted kudzu in the American soil and psyche.

The United States government was seeking an effective way to conserve soil, and kudzu seemed to fit the bill perfectly. The vine was touted as a "wonder plant," a near miracle of nature, and the Department of Agriculture used the Civilian Conservation Corps of the 1930s to distribute and plant the seeds everywhere. Over one hundred million kudzu seeds were planted, and the government actually paid farmers to cultivate it in their fields. They thought, once the soil was healthfully restored, that farmers could just plow over it and return to planting cotton, soybean, or corn.

Yet, kudzu could not be gotten rid of so easily. No one knew that the greatest "wonder" of this plant was its exponential, unstoppable growth. Kudzu, a gift that keeps giving, can now be found throughout North America, including more than thirty US states and parts of Canada.

Nowhere is kudzu's reach more pervasive, however, than in my home region of the American Southeast. It is impossible to drive more than a few miles down a Georgia highway or a Mississippi back road without seeing kudzu smothering road signs, telephone poles, barns, pine tree thickets, school baseball fields, and even the sleepy farmer who takes an afternoon nap too close to the woods. With an ideal climate for its slithery vines, kudzu has climbed, coiled and crept its way across millions of acres of Southern land, changing the countryside forever.

Kudzu has also invaded and weaved its way into Southern culture. It is now as much a part of our shared experience as homemade biscuits, sweet tea, and Baptist church steeples. Thus, we have adapted. We shade our porches with it, feed it to our livestock, use it as a dye, and make baskets with it. We brew it, ferment it, spray it, cut it, mow it, and curse it; but there is one thing we cannot do: ignore it. It has overrun our world, and it is here to stay.

"The kingdom of God is like kudzu planted in a Georgia field."

Would Jesus have said such a thing? Yes, I believe so, because he said something similar to his original listeners with his first story about the reign of God. With picturesque description rather than detailed explanation, Jesus provides a sketch for how the "God Movement"5 works itself out in today's world by saying, "The kingdom of God is like a tiny mustard seed . . . like yeast used in making bread."

Jesus was saying much more than, "The kingdom of God starts small but ends big." Rather, he is telling us that the kingdom of God has intrusive, invasive, takeover qualities about it. Illustrated in the mustard seed and the yeast, Jesus makes clear that his rule is a steady, unstoppable, always growing, always persistent force brought to bear in the world.

The mustard of first-century Palestine overgrew and consumed everything around it. Jesus' first listeners knew this just as

Southerners know about kudzu. A farmer who planted mustard in her garden could not turn her back on it for very long. If she did, it would overrun every other vegetable or herb in the field. And yeast worked the same way. Mysteriously, inexplicably to those living before the understandings of microscopic science, the yeast would find its way into the bland, tasteless flour and transform it. They didn't understand how it worked, but they knew that a tiny amount of yeast had a way of overtaking an entire lump of dough. Mustard and yeast overwhelmed and changed the very nature of their surroundings.

So yes, if Jesus were here today, telling his parables to those who would listen, he just might choose kudzu instead of mustard or yeast to characterize the kingdom of God. These three—mustard, yeast, and kudzu—all have the same properties: they quietly overtake the environments into which they are introduced. They transform the landscape in which they are planted. They overrun everything else they touch. From just a few little seedlings, a few microscopic bubbles, or a few sprouting vines, they explode and cannot be stopped. Such is the kingdom of God and the rule of Christ in today's world.

Just let it have its start—in people's hearts, in people's lives, in the midst of this planet's pain and suffering—and the world will, in fact, change. It will be redeemed. It will be revolutionized. The status quo will be insurrected by hope and transformation, as slowly and steadily the God Movement invades this world with certain salvation. This is not high-minded idealism or a feigned quest for utopia. It is a hopeful, defiant trust that God's will indeed will be done and God's kingdom will come, on earth as it is in heaven, deliberately moving across this planet inch by inch and foot by hopeful foot.

This hopefulness, however, is not shared by all who profess faith in Jesus. To hear the faith peddled from many pulpits and seen practiced in many churches today is to witness a form of Christianity that is neutered of its world-changing power. It is a faith that offers people a chance to forget their current pain and suffering (and the suffering of others), a faith that helps the believer sleep at night, and reminds him or her that there are "just a few more weary days before we take our heavenly flight." But this otherworldly faith does very little to inspire and move people to join God's redeeming mission in the world today.

This is tragic because the world cannot bear much longer a Christian faith that sleeps soundly in the confidence that the faithful will soon be evacuated, for the suffering of this world is too great. We cannot rest in our pews, lulled into a catatonic state, while

- there are nearly fifty million refugees dispersed over this planet;

- one hundred forty-five million orphaned children go to bed each night without a parent;

- twenty-five thousand die every day due simply to contaminated water;

- one hundred million of earth's residents live without a home or permanent shelter;

- a million children are trapped in prostitution and sex slavery;

- and three billion people are denied access to a Christian community of any type.

The love of Christ surely compels us to address these conditions with the good news of the kingdom of God, because this good news does more than ready a person's soul for eternity; it serves body and spirit today. We willingly work to transform the present while aligning ourselves with the will of God, trusting him to bring the world a different future, a future that sets the world to right. Thus, we recoil from focusing all of our attention and energy on the "sweet by-and-by" of tomorrow, leaving only the leftovers for those in this world who cannot afford to wait till tomorrow; and we absolutely refuse to deny the hopeful revolutionary power of the kingdom of God for today's world.

A vivid display of this type of denial comes from an unexpected source: a man named Kim Il-Sung. Il-Sung was the "Great Leader" of North Korea for almost fifty years (his son and grandson succeeded him and have perpetuated his savage legacy), but his greatness could not be more falsely defined. Il-Sung led one of the most tyrannical governments and closed societies in world history. He destabilized an entire region with his thirst for war and nuclear weapons. He accrued one of the most atrocious human rights records in recent decades, and he operated massive internment camps for political prisoners. He subjected huge segments of the North Korean population to starvation and dismantled all Christian churches in the country, martyring many of its leaders. And for all this tragedy and injustice, life in North Korea did not have to be this way.

Kim Il-Sung was not raised as a God-hating, church-destroying, human-rights-violating tyrant. He was raised in a Christian family. His grandfather was a prominent pastor, and his father was a church elder. But Kim Il-Sung did not turn to the faith of his fathers. He turned away. Why? Il-Sung answers with these words: "Many people believed that . . . Jesus would save them from their misery on earth; faith in Christ would give them a better life . . . but I thought Christian doctrines were too far off the mark to suit our misery and problems."6

Those are incredible words, almost impossible to believe, coming from the lips and pen of a man who would become one of the darkest figures of the twentieth century. In his assessment, there was a disconnection between the message of the Christian gospel and the suffering of the world. This separation was not the result of Christian hypocrisy or because the Christians that Kim Il-Sung met were poor witnesses. No, it was one of relevance. "Christian doctrines were too far off the mark" to address the misery and problems of the present world. In the oppression and cruelty of his society, a society that desperately needed rescue—and needs rescue as badly or worse today—the gospel was judged too anemic to address life's real troubles. The result in that country is now evil upon evil, and suffering upon suffering; much of it unnecessarily so, as the trajectory set by Kim Il-Sung could have been much different.

Granted, North Korea's founding father was channeling proto-communist Karl Marx. It was Marx who once said, "Religion is the opiate of the people."7 Marx observed that religion had a tranquilizing effect on people, but religion did very little to actually help people. Rather, it acted as a barbiturate, keeping believers and the world trapped in its current state. It pains me to admit this, but for all their evils and inflicted harm, these men rightly articulated what many Christians fail to see: a Christian faith that does not set people free from their bondage or reverse the deplorable conditions of society is of little worth. Faith that leaves people and the status quo unchanged is useless. It's worse than useless, for it aids and abets the misery of the world rather than revolutionizing the world.

Let there be no mistake: Marx and Il-Sung's revolution was a failure—and remains so. From Communism to Capitalism and Humanism to Utopianism, all "isms" fail to transform a society, because they all fail to transform the human condition (and in many cases, the proposed solutions offered by these movements do more eventual harm than good). We don't need more clever ideas or more impassioned application to change the world. What is needed is a redemption that comes from outside of ourselves. What is needed is a divine, healing insurgency whose growth cannot be overcome by this planet's devastating problems or its people's inability. What is needed is exactly what Jesus offers: a revolution that steadily and effectively brings change and hope to the world. So we throw ourselves into the fray of this fractured world, not only because we care and not because of obligation, but because we believe God isn't finished with this world yet—not by a long shot.

You see, I believe that when you wipe the tears from the cheek of a crying child, the kingdom of God comes. When you feed the hungry in the name of Christ, the reign of God begins. When you offer shelter to a battered woman, the mustard seeds are planted. When you show kindness to your neighbor, the yeast mixes into the dough. When you stand up against injustice and right a wrong, the kudzu vines begin to crawl across God's creation. When you point a person out of poverty and indignity, God's nation expands. When you lead a person to the hope and redemption found in Christ, the world takes a step closer toward inundation with grace, love, and redemption.

All these acts—and a million more just like them—make a real difference because we are not simply helping people, but in Jesus' name, we are actually joining God's divine plot to revolutionize a society tiny step by tiny step. No, we can't take in every single orphan, but we could all take in one. Your Bible Study class can't drill wells for every person dying for water in this world, but it could drill a well for one village. Your mission team can't treat every AIDS patient in Africa, but it could provide medicine for a few of them. Your church can't build a house for every homeless person, but it could go build at least one. We can't rescue every refugee or child of prostitution, but we can—we must—save some of them. The gospel demands it of us, for we are not here to occupy space until we are yanked away by God's sky hook. We are here to deliver God's love and hope to a desperate world.

Some time ago I wrote a Bible study curriculum that began with the obscure story of the US Navy S-4 submarine that sank in Cape Cod Bay in the 1920s. A portion of the story goes: "The submarine, with its crew of forty, sank in less than five minutes. It came to rest more than one hundred feet below on the ocean floor. Rescue attempts, though meager and primitive at the time, began at once. But due to impossible weather, it took twenty-four hours for the first diver to descend to the wreckage. As soon as the diver's feet hit the hull, he immediately heard tapping from inside the submarine. Pounding out Morse code on the hull with a hammer, the diver discovered that six crewmen had survived the collision. Efforts were renewed to reach these men before it was too late. But again, the weather would not cooperate. Every attempt at salvation failed. With their air supply dwindling, the six survivors tapped out in Morse code a final haunting question, 'Is there any hope?'"8

The curriculum that contained this story went to press and was distributed many months after it was submitted to my editor. I had largely forgotten about the curriculum and this story in it until I received a letter from a Bible teacher using the materials. The man wrote: "Dear Ronnie: I am a Sunday School teacher. Even now I am sitting here preparing for tomorrow's lesson. What in the world led you to introduce your series of lessons with the story of the S-4 submarine? Was it chance? Do you have a submarine background? Are you a 'bubblehead'? I have to get back to my studying, but thanks for stirring a few memories." The letter was signed by "Bubblehead Bill Whelan, a World War II submariner."

I responded to him kindly, explaining that I had heard the story of the Cape Cod submarine wreck as a boy and had never forgotten it. I also thanked him for adding the word "bubblehead" to my vocabulary (as I had never heard the word used). Several days later he wrote again: "Ronnie, the Sunday School lesson went well. To stimulate the interest of class members, I read your account and then presented the rest of the story, helping to answer the question, 'Is there any hope?' S-4 rescue attempts were abandoned on 24 December 1927 because of stormy weather; that much is true. Three months later, S-4 was raised and towed to Boston for repairs. But in October 1928, S-4 returned to active duty, not in its original capacity, but assigned and equipped as a submarine rescue ship.

"She and her crew spent the next five years developing procedures and equipment to be used to rescue sunken submariners. In 1938 (years after the S-4 crew asked 'Is there any hope?'), that question was answered: the procedures and equipment developed by S-4 were used to rescue thirty-three submariners from the sunken *Squalus*. I suppose God answers our questions, for there was hope then. There is hope today. And there will be hope tomorrow, if we will get on board. Don't you agree?"

Indeed, I do.

Now is the time to get on board and bring hope to the world. Now is the time to enlist in God's redemptive uprising. Now is the time to participate in real change, change that "brings Good News to the poor, releases the captives, opens the eyes of the blind, and sets the oppressed free" (Luke 4:18). Now is the time for the church to live out a faith that is more concerned with putting on the working gloves of service and grace than determining our level of bliss in the afterlife. Now is the time to wake from our sleepy-headed evasions, to see that the kingdom of God is moving across the planet, slow and steady as she goes. Now is the time to join the revolution—the kudzu conspiracy—as the risen Christ transforms people and transforms the world.

Chapter 2

Do No Harm

"The Kingdom of Heaven is like a farmer who planted good seed in his field. But that night as the workers slept, his enemy came and planted weeds among the wheat, then slipped away. When the crop began to grow and produce grain, the weeds also grew. The farmer's workers went to him and said, 'Sir, the field where you planted that good seed is full of weeds! Where did they come from?' 'An enemy has done this!' the farmer exclaimed. 'Should we pull out the weeds?' they asked. 'No,' he replied, 'you'll uproot the wheat if you do. Let both grow together until the harvest. Then I will tell the harvesters to sort out the weeds, tie them into bundles, and burn them, and to put the wheat in the barn.'"

—MATTHEW 13:24–30 (NLT)

I CAN'T SAY EXACTLY how it happened but it did. I accepted a friend's mysterious invitation to attend what he said would be the "greatest Halloween celebration" I would ever experience. He wouldn't share much more than that. So we met for dinner and then traveled deep into the spooky Appalachian hills to where a little Baptist church was hosting, much to my chagrin, a "Hell House." For the uninitiated—and oh, how fortunate you are!—a Hell House, also known as a "Judgment House," is a revivalistic adaptation of a Haunted House.

9

At each Hell House the script is pretty much the same. A small group of attendees is led through the designated area, and there they become witnesses to scenes of violence or tragedy, scenes typically acted out by high school or college students from the local church. These scenes may involve a group of drunken teenagers killed in a car accident, a frat house drug overdose, or a horrid suicide. In that Hell House I was snookered into years ago, the main script revolved around a school shooting complete with copious amounts of fake blood, cracking firearms, screams of panic in the night, and a horde of the dead and dying. The manifestations are many, but the message is always the same: somebody is going to die and go straight to hell.

The attendees, watching behind the rope line, then observe as the dearly departed take their ill-prepared stand before the judgment seat of God. Their souls hang in the balance for only a few seconds (other participants are waiting to see the show), and then they are dragged away by howling, soul-thirsty demons to burn in eternal fire. After all this shock and awe, and with half of the attendees reduced to tears, it creates just the right moment for the Hell House organizers to present a gospel tract or brochure from the church, to give a well-timed altar call to repentance, or to conduct some plain old-fashioned fear mongering.

My friend thought I would benefit from seeing such a thing, hoping that I would lead my own congregation in hosting a Hell House the next Halloween. He was wrong. I'm not a fan of those things, and as soon as the school shooting scenario began to play itself out, I headed to the car.

I know this type of generated fear very well. I grew up with it. No, we never had a Hell House at my church—that would have been far too worldly or not found in the King James Version of the Bible—but hell was a favorite topic of the preachers that stood behind the pulpit each Sunday (and Sunday evening, at Wednesday night prayer meeting, at Vacation Bible School, and revival service in between). I had memorized a portion of Jonathan Edwards' knee-rattling oratory classic, "Sinners in the Hands of an Angry God," well before I was twelve years old, having heard it quoted so often, and I can still hear it ring through the church sanctuary:

"God holds you over the pit of hell, much as one holds a loathsome insect over the fire. . . . There is no other reason to be given, why you have not dropped into hell since you arose this morning. O sinner! Consider the fearful danger you are in: You hang by a slender thread."9

None of this preaching comforted or encouraged me. It did not make me "a better Christian." It did not make me long for heaven (who wanted to be with such an irritated God, anyway). No, it made me half-crazy, more in need of hospitalization and an injection of Thorazine than I needed another admonition to "escape the fires of hell prepared for the devil and his angels, where the fire is not quenched, the worm dieth not, and the smoke of that pit rises up forever and ever" (I still remember the oft-invoked warnings).

Hell was real, hell was hot, hell was forever, and I was in danger of going there right quick and in a hurry. The only way to avoid this horrible fate was to accept Jesus as my personal Lord and Savior. I did so with gusto, or as Bill Leonard described some conversions: "We were saved hard, sweating like we had been to hell that morning and come back to the revival to tell about it that night."10 That was me; and the best I could tell, the only reason for Jesus and the entire church operation—the whole meaning of the Christian life—was to evade hell and a very angry God who wanted people to go there pronto.

A favorite text of the fire-and-brimstone preachers of my childhood was this second kingdom parable of Jesus, a parable commonly referred to as "The Parable of the Wheat and the Tares." Why was it so beloved? Well, it is so apparently black and white. Some are "in," some are "out." There is sure joy and definite punishment. Some will make it through heaven's gates, but most will be sent to the fire. This parable was (and remains) a phenomenal revivalistic tool, giving full-throated endorsement to the "accept-Jesus-to-escape-hell" gospel.

Yet, I don't think that Jesus told this parable to prove that "there is nothing between you and hell but the air."11 This is not a story that Jesus provided evangelists so that they would have means and motive to manipulate people down the aisle to the mourner's bench. Rather, this is a parable about living a fruitful life *now*. At the risk of oversimplification, this parable is about our role in the world today; it is about blooming and growing where we are planted, bearing the fruit of the kingdom of God. Yes, the gospel is a gospel of urgency, but the urgent need is to respond to Christ's call "to bear much fruit" in the world, a world desperate for healing.

To the parable at hand, Jesus confirms that there are two kinds of plants growing in the soil that is this world. First, there are the good plants sprung from good seed, the children of the kingdom of God. They will one day be harvested and brought into the Master's barn. Second, there are the bad plants sprung from bad seed, sown by the devil himself. These will one day be harvested as well, but these wiry, thistly thorns will be cast on the trash heap. I use that term—trash heap—intentionally, as it seems to communicate most clearly Jesus' idea (see Matthew 13:42).

The most often translated word for "hell" in the New Testament is the word *gehenna*. Though used in the New Testament, it is a Hebrew word referring to a specific place, here in this world, not necessarily the world to come. *Gehenna* was and is the deep, narrow Valley of Ge Hinnom south of Jerusalem. There, the Palestinian ancients worshiped their fire gods and the idolatrous Jews of the past sacrificed their children to the pagan god Molech. Because of its distasteful past, this place eventually became a landfill, the city dump, where the trash and refuse of Jerusalem was cast. In Jesus' day the bodies of criminals, rejects, and the poor who were without proper burial sites were cast there to rot in the open air. For generations on end, *gehenna* represented everything filthy, rejected, and under judgment.

We are hard-pressed then, to make hell (read *gehenna*) as we have so often accepted it, to be anything different than the city of Jerusalem's landfill—a trash heap—for that is how Jesus used the word. In fact, of the dozen times the word *gehenna* is used in the New Testament, it is Jesus who uses that word exclusively, save one.

So while we could debate and deliberate on *gehenna* (many do) and the nature of hell (many more do that), that is not Jesus' purpose here. He didn't elaborate about it (remember, Jesus rarely explains; nor will I). Again, we are looking for those key characteristics of the kingdom of God, and Jesus insisted that the ultimate outcome of these two very different seeds is not the more important issue of the parable. Rather, the key to interpreting this story is in verses 28-30. The workers ask, "Should we pull out the weeds?" And the answer is given: "No, you'll uproot the wheat if you do. Let both grow together until the harvest."

Good and bad grow side by side in this world. There is evil and there is right. There are those who have joined the gracious and just kingdom of God, and those who work against it. They are intermingled and intertwined, their roots sometimes twisted together. Only the final harvest will untangle and separate these. Jesus makes it clear that the final harvest, what is going to happen at the end of the age, is God's business, not ours. Further, how people live their lives today is God's business as well. As followers of Jesus, we cannot go into the world thinking we know who is "in" and who is "out" (the whole point of much of today's preaching), who is a bad thistle and who the good seed is. We cannot make it our vocation to root out evil. If we do that, we will do far more harm than good. We will hurt the work of God's kingdom if we focus on purging those things and people who appear to be invaders in the field in which we have been planted.

The separatists in some strains of our faith must object here: "Wait! If we don't dig out or purge some of this evil, if we continue to allow the good and the bad to be twisted together, don't we risk being contaminated with the wrong type of people?" Yes, absolutely, but that is the way it should be! We have to run that risk. It is our vocation, as light of the world and salt of the earth, to graciously mingle with all people, displaying grace, justice, and compassion, while leaving all judgments to God. The only assignment we have been given is to simply bloom and flourish where we have been planted, less concerned with who we might condemn, and more concerned with leading whole, fruitful lives that reflect the glory of heaven on earth. Our prayer must be: "Lord, help us not to sort, categorize, uproot, judge, or otherwise do harm to those around us. Lord, just help us to grow where we are planted, and as we grow, spread love to all in the fields that surround us."

Consistently, and this should rend our hearts to pieces, Christians are characterized as mean-spirited, judgmental, critical, and inflexible (you don't have to attend a hell-obsessed church or need research statistics to confirm this conclusion; simply do an informal interview on any street corner). This is a reputation we have largely earned, because we communicate from places of fear and threat. We hold the ignited fires of God's judgment over people's heads and beneath our neighbors' feet. We have been more concerned with proving how right we are and how those who are wrong are going to face judgment, than we have been concerned with living out God's profound love and grace found in Jesus Christ.

It is always possible, and this is a real danger for followers of Jesus, to become so hardened in our convictions about hell (what it is/how long it will last/who is going there), that the only purpose the gospel has for us and for those with whom we share, is avoiding the fiery inferno. The gospel is reduced to a fire insurance policy, and when that happens, the gospel is emasculated of its transforming power to change people today.

As an example, for years a friend of mine worked for a Christian community organization that attempted to help the poor. A portion of this work involved a food bank; a much needed place in the community where hungry people could come and get a few groceries for their families. It was superb, and when I was invited to be a part of it, I volunteered at this food bank right away. My intention was to sort cans and boxes, meet some nice people, and lend a hand to those who were hungry. It wasn't a Mother Teresa feat, but to give a cup of cold water (or a box of spaghetti noodles) to someone thirsty or hungry is to serve Christ himself (more about that in the pages to come).

But when I arrived at the distribution site I was given the assignment of "counselor" along with a name badge to prove it. I was, after all, a "pastoral type," and who better to fulfill the required faith counseling for those coming to acquire food? You see, before anyone departed with the bounty of brown bags, he or she was required to see a counselor. No counseling, no food; it was that simple. This counseling consisted of sitting on a cold metal chair in a room the size of a closet, under flickering fluorescent lights, while being force-fed a gospel tract. The promised groceries sat, tauntingly, in the corner the entire time. As if a person having to ask for food wasn't dignity-killing enough, now the needy person had to be subjected to having his or her empty stomach used against them.

This is not a behavior isolated to hell-fire-and-damnation preaching and cajoling food banks. Christians are very good at this sort of thing. In shadow and mold-laden church basements, in college dorms and church buses, in the inner city, on country roads, and on international soil, little evangelistic teams come together huddling commando-style around their maps, holding hands, and saying their prayers. Sufficiently locked and loaded, they launch attacks on their neighbors asking questions like, "If you were to die tonight and stand before God, why should he let you into his heaven?" or "Are you sure that, if you should die today, that you will definitely go to heaven?" These questions are asked with the ultimate ambition of getting the respondent to dodge hell and hit heaven, and with such a noble goal the questionable means are rarely examined.

It amounts to what Roger Williams equated with "raping the soul;" manipulation toward a spiritual decision. That's a stout assessment for what sometimes happens beneath the flickering fluorescent lights of a food bank or "witnessing" on the front steps of a targeted convert's home, but it is an assessment that is correct. Whether it is physical, spiritual, or emotional damage, the gospel should not—cannot—it must not—be used to hurt or harm others. We must abandon our militant approach in sharing our faith; we have to quit cornering people, demanding immediate decisions, and using emotionally charged environments to wrangle decisions.

Should we share and live our faith? Yes! But I believe that every person is capable of relating directly to God without coercion or interference by others. Every person should be given the right of free choice in his or her relationship with God (or without God). Every individual should be given the respect and the dignity as image-bearing creations of God to arrive at his or her own spiritual conclusions, choosing to be Catholic or Coptic, Methodist or Muslim, Buddhist or Baptist, Jew or Jainist, Anglican or atheist, without heavy-handedness of any kind. As that great old Baptist from Oklahoma, Herschel Hobbs, put it: "The Church cannot fasten its iron grip upon a man's soul. This deprives him of his greatest dignity—the right of free choice in his relationship to God. This is the worst of all tyrannies. And it is made worse by its claim to be in the name of God who created men and women to be free."12 We need to learn to give others space and grace to others, for this is God's field and God's work. We have only joined him in that work.

What does this space and grace look like? One such approach, and one consistent with this parable I think, is a phrase I have heard some Mennonites use, an approach they call "nonviolent evangelism."13 It is a way of respectfully sharing faith that does not harm those with whom they share. It is built on mutual respect, love for others, and a commitment to the other person's freedom. People are treated as seekers, not potential converts, without pressure, arm-twisting or coercion, and no manipulation of words or emotions. Such seekers are not vilified, targeted, pursued, or argued with. They are simply invited into radical hospitality where questions and exploration are not only tolerated, but encouraged and expected. These nonviolent evangelists share their faith with a "come and see" attitude, opening their arms and hearts to others, leaving the rest to God.

Here is an example. My friend Sabrina and her husband Blake live in a Christian community on a working farm. By "Christian community," I mean a group of people who are attempting to live out the way of Jesus while sharing life, space, and the same values. It's not a commune—Sabrina, Blake, and the other two dozen folks living there are definite individuals—it is a community: a group of people helping the world and welcoming others in the name of Christ. Welcome, in fact, is what brought Sabrina to the farm. She wasn't a Christian when she arrived. Actually, she was agnostic and at times rather hostile toward faith. But she loved the earth, she was trying to stay sober, and she and Blake wanted to give self-sustaining, organic farming a try while they were still young enough to pull it off.

Through a series of inexplicable events, but mostly because of the dramatic welcome others at the farm gave them, this couple found themselves moving out of the city and into the cornfields. Sabrina was going to farm the land with gusto, but she had no intention of getting involved with what she called "that Jesus stuff." And her co-farmers respected that. But one day, after being surrounded by all this grace and love, and having begun to pray again and study the way of Jesus, she woke up in half panic, half celebration, and all surprise: "Oh, my God, I think I'm a Christian!" It was a beautiful conversion, one made possible by giving plenty of margin not manipulation, offering help and not inflicting harm.

Maybe it is because I have been greatly influenced in recent years by the Mennonites, because I long ago defied my own coercive religious upbringing, because I believe that a gospel focused exclusively on hell-evasion is a gospel run amok, or because of precious people like Sabrina, but I have come to the core conclusion that we need to give people some breathing and growing room. We must back off, show respect, leave room for God's grace, and exchange the tactics of fear, threat, and anger for the quiet, simple, fruitful life in Christ. This is a life of "love, joy, peace, patience, kindness, goodness, faithfulness, gentleness and self-control" toward all people with whom we come in contact. It is a life that has a way of germinating and sprouting its way into the field in which it is planted.

Chapter 3

The Pearl of the World

"The Kingdom of Heaven is like a treasure that a man discovered hidden in a field. In his excitement, he hid it again and sold everything he owned to get enough money to buy the field. Again, the Kingdom of Heaven is like a merchant on the lookout for choice pearls. When he discovered a pearl of great value, he sold everything he owned and bought it!"

—MATTHEW 13:44-46 (NLT)

JOHN STEINBECK WAS ONE of America's most prolific and insightful writers. Renowned for his prize-winning works that most of us either enjoyed or endured at some point in our education (depending upon our perspective), one of Steinbeck's lesser known novellas is my personal favorite. It is a penetrating little book called *The Pearl*.

Steinbeck's story begins with a poor Mexican pearl diver and fisherman named Kino, who ekes out a living for his wife and infant son with a little canoe and a thatch hut on the beach. When Kino's son is bitten by a scorpion, the white, wealthy doctor will not see the child, for Kino has no money. Nor will the priest come to pray for the child, because Kino and his wife aren't properly married— again, because Kino can't afford to pay the church for a proper wedding ceremony. Kino is left with his own prayers and begs the gods to grant him the grace to find a great pearl, whereby he can pay for his son to be healed, his marriage to be blessed, and for his own escape from the village.

Kino's prayers are answered. While diving, he discovers a pearl as big as his fist: the "Pearl of the World," the locals call it, the most incredible treasure the village has ever seen. Now Kino will be rich. He and his wife will be properly married. His son will be healed. The family will get new clothes and a larger house. His life will be transformed. But, things don't work out as well as Kino had hoped.

Greed takes over the village and Kino's own heart. Thieves attempt to rob him of his success. Callously, the pearl traders refuse to buy the treasure from him. His friends grow psychotically jealous. Kino begins to spend all his energies hiding and protecting his treasure. His wife, who sees how the new wealth is destroying their family, tries to get rid of the pearl, only to have Kino viciously attack her. More robbers burn their house down. They are forced to run for their lives while the would-be assassins mercilessly stalk the family like prey. Yet, Kino cannot let this pearl go. He cries out in desperation: "What can I do? This pearl has become my soul!"14

In the end Kino loses everything: his home, his young child, his little canoe by which he made a living, his respectability in the village, and his ability to escape to a better life. He and his wife stand on the Pacific shoreline and heave the evil pearl back into the ocean. It breaks him, having caused nothing but sorrow and loss. Steinbeck's story is about one getting the treasure that one wants, only to discover that the treasure is one's undoing. It is a story about the little dog that finally catches the school bus, but then realizes that he can't do anything with it. It is a story in which we have all played the lead character.

We all enter this world with empty hands, open hearts, and restless spirits searching for some kind of treasure—something to fill the emptiness. The search is intrinsic, natural and good. The glitch in all of our pursuits is that many of the things we seek do not actually fulfill us. In fact, many of our pursuits have the opposite effect. They are detrimental to us and to the world. My guess is that the majority of individual and cosmic suffering is the direct result of our improper and misguided searches. The itchiness in our hands and in our hearts sends us looking for an emotional and spiritual scratching post, but we entrust ourselves to people and objects that simply cannot deliver the goods. Our search goes off the rails, and we end up with terribly destructive counterfeits.

Here is an axiom that governs life: if you are not looking for the right thing, you will probably miss it when it comes along. And here is the axiom's corollary: if you are not looking for the right thing, you will certainly settle for the wrong thing.

Jesus offers a solution for our search. He sends us off in the right direction looking for the right thing. This solution is illustrated in two kingdom stories known as "The Hidden Treasure" and "The Pearl of Great Price." The first involves a poor itinerant farmer who happens upon a treasure trove in the field he is plowing. The second is about a merchant on an intentional pursuit for the "Pearl of the World." These are two very different men from two very different social and economic classes who discover the kingdom of God in two completely different ways.

One stubs his toe and stumbles over a surprising grace that he never saw coming. The other one travels the world knowing that "it" was out there somewhere if he could just find it. As different as their journeys and stations in life are, they come to the same conclusion: the treasure in their hands is the end of all their searching. This discovery changes their lives. Jesus says, "The kingdom of God is like this." It is completely and totally fulfilling—if we will receive it into our empty hands.

To the first parable: in the days when Jesus first told this story about a hidden treasure, there were no banking systems as we know them today, so people did not put their valuables in a safe deposit box in a bank down on Main Street or lock them up in a vault at the community credit union. The most common practice was to stuff their coins or their keepsakes into an earthen jar, and then bury it somewhere on their land. This wasn't an act of carelessness, as if they were leaving their most prized possession just lying around; it was the most responsible thing the owners of these treasures could do. The man in Jesus' story, most likely a hired day laborer, finds just such a treasure buried in a field as he goes about his day of working the ground.

To imagine what such a discovery would look like, consider the assessment of Gerhard Lenski. Lenski has written extensively about ancient agrarian societies, as was Palestine's in the first century, showing that such cultures were rife with obscene levels of inequality.15 There were essentially two classes with the rulers, bureaucrats, priests, and merchants on the "upper side" of society. These people had all the means, money, and stability. Then, across a gulf so wide it was impossible to see the other side, much less cross it, was the lower class.

In this lower class were the peasants (the vast majority of the population), the artisans, and those who had a trade (like Jesus who was a carpenter and was considered lower than a peasant). Below these were the unclean like tax collectors, prostitutes, "sinners," and Gentiles. And then, the lowest level of all, were those called "The Expendable." These were thieves, con men, street people, and what Lenski calls, "Itinerant workers forced to live solely by their wits or charity."16 This seems to be the man in Jesus' parable, for he is not the landowner. He is an itinerant worker at the bottom of the social ladder of his day.

So imagine that the man rises early in the morning after sleeping in his Kino-like hut. He wakes, not so much because it is morning, but because his stomach is growling and so are the stomachs of his children. His throat is parched with thirst, his only water being a mud hole just off the main street. And even then he has to fight the feral dogs away just to get a sip of it. He uses some of the stagnant water to "clean" the grime off his face, he adjusts the rags on his back that serve as his clothes, and aching from sleeping on a reed mat, he limps down to the market hoping someone will hire him for a few dollars and a little breakfast. Miracle of miracles, he lands a job! He will live to fight for at least one more day, and maybe feed his family. He is taken to a field and put to work tilling row after endless row with a dull plow pulled by a stubborn ox, just about as thin as he is. It is hot, dusty, monotonous work.

At some point in the dullness of the afternoon, the sun beating down on his hatless head, the plow strikes what he thinks is a rock. Mainly because his boredom has been broken, he gives the "rock" another poke with his bare foot. But it's not a rock; it's a jar. The man's pulse quickens, and he peeks around to see if he is alone. He ties the ox's reins in a knot, drops to his knees, and begins clawing

21

the earth with his fingers. The sweat is dropping off his brow and into the dirt; his fingers begin to bleed because the jar is well impacted and heavy. Finally, the jar emerges, not much larger than a melon. He pops the lid off and nearly faints when he looks inside. He was hoping the jar had an old lady's necklace or maybe—just maybe—a few coins forgotten by a past owner. No, he finds it running over with gold, silver, and precious stones! He was just trying to survive, just trying to make enough money to live one more day, and now he uncovers this avalanche of grace and wealth!

He is the squeegee man on the street who takes home a pair of jeans given to him by the rescue mission, only to discover that the winning lottery ticket is in the pocket of those jeans.

He is the homemaker who goes shopping at the thrift store because money is tight, and she buys a cute little china set only to find out it is from the Ming Dynasty and is worth hundreds of thousands of dollars.

He is the prospector coming home from the Klondike, busted and broke, not even a shovel left to trade. As he hitchhikes home he stumbles alongside the road, only to look down and see the rock he spilled himself over is a gold nugget weighing fifteen pounds.

Here is the kingdom of God: it is a discovery that completely, totally, fully, fundamentally, and absolutely changes a person's life. It is a deliverance that one never thought possible, brought to all of its radical, liberating, and gracious fulfillment.

How did the worker in the field "get in on" all of this? It wasn't difficult. His hands were already empty (he probably had to go beg, borrow, and steal to buy the field). This is why Jesus uses this particular man in his story, I think. Remember his status in society. He is less than a nobody, an "expendable." When he found this vast treasure he had no real choice to make, for as a pauper, it was easy to take hold of the treasure when he discovered it. He needed only to acknowledge that his hands were empty, and then his life was completely satisfied. As Simone Weil wrote so accurately, "Grace fills empty spaces, but it can only enter where there is a void to receive it."17

This type of emptiness is an absolute requirement for receiving the gospel. This is why, it seems, Jesus makes a subtle but important change in his storytelling. As the short tale of the "Hidden Treasure" concludes, onto the stage walks the pearl merchant who is seeking "choice pearls." Remember from Lenski's earlier assessment the place this new character occupies in the society of his day. As a merchant who buys, sells, and trades in precious stones, he is in the upper class. He is on the opposite side of the tracks from the man in Jesus' earlier story. Yet, to lay his hands on the discovered treasure, this merchant takes exacting steps to become as empty and poor as the itinerant, obscure worker in the field. He sells everything—everything—to satisfy his search. And for the pearl merchant, this was a far more difficult task than it was for the humble farm worker.

By never having had the opportunity to fill his life with the things that might distract him from discovering God's real treasure, the poor farmer was, in fact, at a decided advantage over the pearl merchant. The farmer had very little to relinquish. He had only to receive, while the merchant had to give up his very life before he could take hold of the new life laid out before him. It is no wonder that Jesus said, "God blesses those who are poor and realize their need for him." He said this, not to glorify poverty, but to show that the only receptacle for God's grace is a vacant human heart. "The kingdom of heaven is theirs," Jesus concludes (Matthew 5:3), emphasizing that the kingdom is unattainable by those who are not empty and humble enough to simply receive.

Certainly this puts the farmer in a more favorable position than the merchant in Jesus' parable, and most of us, for we live in a culture where "success" is of the utmost importance. Wouldn't we all prefer to be a pearl merchant making a comfortable living rather than an itinerant worker on the constant brink of starvation? Absolutely! Such a contrast is laughable if we miss the point Jesus is making: we all must become poor in one way or another to experience life within the kingdom of God.

Yet, we are our own worst enemies (just like Steinbeck's character, Kino). Our good old Protestant work ethic (Catholics work just as hard, by the way) drives us to amass everything from fortunes and followers to perfect attendance pins and pats on the back. Whether our accomplishments are material, social, religious, educational, or in some other field, the danger remains the same:

we can become so full of ourselves that there is no room left for anything else.

Achievement should be rightly celebrated, yes, but it cannot be forgotten that egotism, pride, and ambition are the real enemies of the gospel. Why? Because when our hands, heads, and hearts are full, we are simply unable to accept what God wants to give us. In the words of Leo Tolstoy, "Even the strongest current of water cannot add a drop to a cup which is already full."18

For example, there's an old story about a scholar who climbed the storied mountain to meet the Zen Master face to face and to learn from him. This scholar had an extensive academic background. He had read and studied all the important texts and was a wealth of knowledge and experience. After making all the customary bows and introductions, the two sat together and the scholar began talking about all he had done, all he had studied, and all he hoped to achieve in the future. The Master listened carefully and patiently and began to brew tea for the two to share.

When the tea was ready, the Master brought it over and began gently pouring it in the scholar's cup; and he kept pouring, pouring, and pouring. It filled the cup, ran over into the saucer, into the scholar's lap and onto the floor!

The scholar jumped up shouting, "Stop! Stop! The cup is full and running over; you can't get any more in there!"

The Master stopped pouring and said, "Yes, and you are just like this cup. You are so full of yourself that nothing else can get in! You come here asking to be taught, but I can teach you nothing until your cup is empty."

I say this explicitly: none of us will discover the kingdom of God or experience any lasting satisfaction in this world so long as we remain full of ourselves. The gospel is completely unappealing— it is downright repulsive—to those of us who feel that we can manage our lives with our own abilities, resources, accomplishments, or on our own terms. As long as this self-reliance reigns supreme, the reign of God cannot take root in our lives.

Thus, we find that the pearl merchant may have been a recipient of even greater grace than the poor farmer. Clearly, the farmer stumbled and bumbled his way onto a treasure, but the merchant found the ability to boldly and recklessly abandon all he had and all he had previously known. Such an act of courageous and willing sacrifice is not "normal." Rather, it is nothing less than a divine intervention. Returning to Simone Weil's earlier quote, and completing her thought, she summarizes the merchant's ability to release his life concisely: "Grace fills empty spaces, but it can only enter where there is a void to receive it; *and it is grace itself which makes this void*" (emphasis added).19 The merchant received the grace to exchange his previous life for the life now put before him, and the "Pearl of the World" became his.

The merchant learned what I hope God gives us all the grace to learn:

- Emptiness is not a curse; it is the cure.

- Insufficiency is not the end; it is the beginning.

- Admitting that our hands hold nothing is not a liability; it is receptivity.

- When we are exhausted with nothing else to give, that is at last, a prayer for our life to be transformed.

As a conclusion for this chapter, consider my dear friend, Michael Bonderer. At the time of this writing he is a Christian missionary in El Salvador with an organization called "Homes from the Heart," a not-for-profit that has built hundreds of homes and sheltered thousands of poor and forgotten families in the last decade. Michael has been guiding the work every step of the way. Michael is not your typical missionary. He sort of came to the task by accident. He is a nicotine-addicted, four-letter-word-dropping, endless-coffee-drinker of a man who says he has "done everything wrong." But he is also a wise sage, a deeply committed follower of Jesus, and a believer in redemption, whose work testifies to so much that has been done right.

Michael is older and more fragile now, a survivor of lung cancer, multiple heart attacks, quadruple bypass surgery, a stroke in the Honduran mountains, and a three-pack-a-day habit. Yet, for all that he has survived, and the housing ministry he has led, his greatest accomplishment is this: he has changed. He has been clean and sober—a recovering alcoholic—for more than thirty years. And whether he floundered his way into recovery or chased it down like a man on a mission, it is impossible to say. Maybe it was a little of both. All I know is that he traded his life that was a dead end for what God offered, and he has never been the same—and neither has the world around him.

Once on a visit to the United States, Michael took me to his Alcoholics Anonymous (AA) hall in Kansas City to meet a few of his old friends and to show me where his life turned around. This AA hall is and has been the consummate meeting place for drunks, coke-heads, Al-Anons, over-eaters, sexaholics, and addicts of all shades and stripes. Hundreds, if not thousands of people have passed through that place on their way—God willing—to some kind of healing change. And, like Michael, they keep going back: going back to the AA hall, and more importantly, going back to the "First Step" in the recovery process.

That "First Step," jotted down by AA Founders Bill Wilson and Dr. Bob Smith so many years ago, is the admission of emptiness: we "admit that we are powerless and that our lives have become unmanageable." It is the confession that we have nothing left in our hands and nothing left to give. We must let go of the life we have lived—for our searching has resulted in a dead end—so that a new life can be lived. None of the transformational change in my friend Michael's life—and none of the change that has blessed the world through him—would have been possible without him coming to the end of himself and admitting his helplessness.

While Michael is an unusual and unique man to say the least, his struggles and problems are not. This world is shattered and spilling over with people who are shattered and spilling over; with people whose stumblings and searches have ended in colossal disaster; with people who have given up all hope and prospects for life to be any different than it is for them right now. But just like Michael, such people are the perfect candidates for transformation—if they will have it—for when the brokenness of individuals and of our world collides with God's free and abundant grace, then radical change becomes possible.

When we acknowledge that we have nothing left, it is then that we have found the most important thing of all: the capacity to accept grace when it is offered to us. Such grace truly is "The Pearl of the World"; it is the glad end to all of our searching. And it is the gospel that can bring fulfillment to people right here and right now.

Chapter 4

"The Little Way"

After they arrived at Capernaum and settled in a house, Jesus asked his disciples, "What were you discussing out on the road?" But they didn't answer, because they had been arguing about which of them was the greatest. He sat down, called the twelve disciples over to him, and said, "Whoever wants to be first must take last place and be the servant of everyone else." Then he put a little child among them. Taking the child in his arms, he said to them, "Anyone who welcomes a little child like this on my behalf welcomes me, and anyone who welcomes me welcomes not only me but also my Father who sent me."

—MARK 9:33–37 (NLT)

One day some parents brought their children to Jesus so he could touch and bless them. But the disciples scolded the parents for bothering him. When Jesus saw what was happening, he was angry with his disciples. He said to them, "Let the children come to me. Don't stop them! For the Kingdom of God belongs to those who are like these children. I tell you the truth, anyone who doesn't receive the Kingdom of God like a child will never enter it."

—MARK 10:13–15 (NLT)

WHEN SENATOR AND FORMER Governor of Georgia Zell Miller gave an impassioned speech at the Republican National

Convention a few years ago, it was an historic and controversial event. Miller had crossed party lines to give it, he being a lifelong Democrat. Shortly afterwards, with his words still echoing in Madison Square Garden, he granted an interview with television reporter Chris Matthews, an interview that became even more historic and controversial than his Convention speech.20 Zell became furious in the course of the interview and said to Matthews, "You know, I wish we lived in the day where you could challenge a person to a duel!" And he meant it. It was a stunning piece of political theater.

Now, what made old "Give 'em Hell Zell" (as he's known in my native Georgia) so incredibly angry? It went beyond politics, policy, or some huge philosophical disagreement. It was this: Zell Miller felt that his honor had been assaulted. He had not been merely disagreed with, but he concluded that Chris Matthews had insolently mocked him. In short, he felt disrespected. For a man of the Southern Highlands, there is no greater transgression than that. To show disrespect to someone who feels he or she deserves respect is truly a duel-worthy offense.

My neighbor Zell Miller could be the poster child for an entire series of debated cultural studies on this phenomenon. It's called the "culture of honor," a societal mindset that places high value on defending one's reputation at all costs. Researchers say that, here in America, there is one particular area of the country more shaped by the "culture of honor" than any other: the Appalachian South.

Southern Appalachia was settled primarily by the Scott-Irish (immigrants from Scotland and North Ireland), who came from the farms of Ulster in the 1700s. They found in the Appalachians what was already familiar to them: small, rocky outcrops on the edge of the frontier where space was limited and resources even more so. Reducing the research to the extreme, these hardy pioneers who were crammed into tight quarters developed a fierce "Don't tread on me" attitude. This attitude was the product of suspiciously guarding their resources and boundaries, just as their shepherding forefathers had done in the old country. The often uneasy peace was kept by practicing respect, courtesy and honor. Should a neighbor show disrespect, much less a liberal television reporter from the Northeast, it was a personal assault on one's standing in the community and regarded as a preemptive strike to take advantage of one's place and resources. Disrespect, therefore, could not go unchallenged.

The volatility of such an "honor society" is most graphically illustrated in the historical family feuds of Appalachia. Families with legendary names like O'Shields and Vandiver; Howard and Turner; Martin and Tolliver; and of course the Hatfields and McCoys, spilled gallons of blood over the decades as they waged war for generations. And in most cases, these feuds began over some social slight, some minor affront or disregard that demanded an apology or atonement that never materialized. Thus, Zell Miller is a product of his cultural and historical environment.21 He was conditioned to respond to dishonor, even on national television, with a literal vengeance.

But it doesn't end with Zell Miller's generation. Such conditioning continues, well beyond the family feuds of yesteryear and Southern pride. Believe it or not, murder rates are higher in the friendly Appalachian South of America than anywhere else in the country. Yet, such violence is hardly ever committed against strangers. As John Shelton Reed has said, "The homicides in which the South [specializes] are those in which someone is being killed by someone he or she knows, and for reasons that both the killer and the victim understand."22 In other words, the violence is almost always personal, a crime of vengeful passion as one seeks to protect his or her honor, again, at all costs.

For the descendants of these mountain pioneers (Millers and McBrayers included), this is a cultural legacy we have inherited and propagated, just as surely as our slow, hardened accents. And despite the fact that Southern Appalachia is also one of the most religious areas of the country, and has some of the highest church attendance rates, for generations my ancestors and neighbors have missed a major component of the Christian faith: an honor-protecting society is incompatible with the kingdom of God, and our cultural legacy of protecting reputation at all costs is on a collision course with the way of Jesus.

Jesus said, "Whoever wants to be first must take last place and be the servant of everyone else," and "anyone who doesn't receive the Kingdom of God like a child will never enter it." Whatever God's kingdom is, you can be sure of this: it is not an honor society as we understand honor. It is a community where individuals willingly relinquish their rights and their egos. It is not about the protection of personal space, resources, and reputation. It is the practice of giving up, giving in, and giving over. It is not a duel to see who is left standing. It is a lifestyle of service to others. It is not about the heroic ascent to the top, but about the humble descent to the bottom.

Yes, we have discovered in Jesus' kingdom parables a powerful and vital way to live in the current world. It is a way of life that is revolutionary in its power and transformative in its scope. Yet, it only becomes available to us by means of grace, a grace received as we empty ourselves to accept what God offers. If we who are Christian cannot be converted to this—if smallness and humility cannot replace our own culture of egoism, self-importance, and ruthless rivalry—then the movement of God in Jesus has little chance of impacting our world.

Jesus reinforces this theme in the twin texts that form the foundation for this chapter. Real change, for the individual and the world, is possible when we reduce ourselves, rather than promote ourselves. Paraphrasing the words of Meister Eckhart, the way of Jesus has "much more to do with subtraction, than it does addition."23

Taking up the texts, it's easy to see that this is not a traditional parable of Jesus. It's more of a living metaphor or a symbol of how life within the kingdom of God is lived. The texts involve two episodes, separated by an unknown but likely short time frame, and both episodes include children to reveal how abysmally off-course Jesus' disciples were in their thinking. (The Appalachian South's culture has no monopoly on feuding and jockeying for power. It is a large part of being human.) They, like us, completely missed the point with regard to what Jesus' radical movement was all about.

First, the disciples were walking along the road having what they thought was a private debate, and Jesus asked, "What were you arguing about as we walked along the road?" They immediately clammed up because they had been arguing over who was going to be the greatest in Jesus' coming administration. Who was going to be second-in-command? Who was going to be Secretary of State? Who was going to be ambassador to Egypt? We know that James and John openly asked to share the greatest spot in the kingdom at one point. We know that Peter was the self-proclaimed leader. Matthew was probably the most educated. Judas had the money, and money is power. And Simon was a political zealot who probably understood the most effective use of military force. There was a lot of competition among them and a great deal of respect and honor at stake. You can hear the swords being sharpened and the dueling pistols being loaded.

The second episode is similar. A few days later Jesus is teaching and healing when parents begin bringing their children to him for a blessing, a common rabbinical practice. What did the disciples do? They turned the children away. More so, they ran them off. They guarded Jesus, not because they thought these parents and children could harm him, but because they felt that Jesus (and thusly they as well) was too important and doing far too important work to be bothered by the little people. "Run along now," they said, "we have no time for such minor inconveniences."

In both episodes Jesus rebukes the disciples with a healthy dose of anger. The word in Mark 10, where it says "Jesus became angry," is a word that means "to be bent or to curve." Literally, the attitude and behavior of the disciples got Jesus bent out of shape. They were going in the wrong direction—completely—and they just didn't get it. Their density astounded and angered him.

So, he takes corrective measures, measures that overturn their sense of honor and respectability. He plants a child right in the middle of their squabbling and their self-important agendas and says, "You have to turn around." That is, you have to stop going in the direction you are going, "and become like a child, become like a slave."

Certainly Jesus was speaking Aramaic when he said these words, and here, his language is significant. In Aramaic the word for "child" and the word for "slave" is the same: *talya*. Jesus wasn't idealizing slavery or childhood. He wasn't exalting a slave's chains or emphasizing a child's innocence. No, Jesus was pointing to the *status* of a *talya*. "If you want to get in on this thing," Jesus says, "you don't get there by clawing your way to top. You have to become unimportant. You have to descend to the lowest possible place in the social strata. You have to get small to fit through the door that leads to the kingdom of God."

Be sure, this isn't some kind of over-played Puritanism or a self-critical, debasing "for a worm such as I" kind of attitude. (That's an inverted pride in and of itself that celebrates one's depravity.) No, this is simply humility. It's an attitude whereby we don't think badly of ourselves; we simply don't think of ourselves at all. We relinquish our rights, our demands, our striving, and our struggles, and yes, the sense of honor and respect that we think we deserve. Quoting Jesus again: "If you put yourself above others, you will be put down. But if you humble yourself, you will be honored" (see Luke 14).

Such humility is exhibited in an original, mythical tale about a young man named Walter, who went to work for the largest corporation in the world.24 The personnel director told Walter that he must start at the bottom and work his way up, for that is the way one succeeds. So Walter, not afraid of hard work, began his corporate career in the mailroom, in the basement of the building. Walter liked his job, but he often daydreamed about what it would be like to be a person of power, an executive, the president of the company, or maybe even the chairman of the board.

One day as Walter was dividing and sorting the mail, he saw a cockroach in the corner of the room. He was disgusted, so he walked over to step on it. It was then that a tiny voice cried up to him, "Don't kill me, Walter! I'm Milton the Cockroach, and if you spare me I will grant you all your wishes." Well, what was Walter to do? It's not every day one comes across a talking cockroach, so he spared the bug's life. And to test the ability of his new-found friend, Walter wished to leave the mailroom and become vice president of the company. "Do that for me," Walter said, "and I will let you live."

Walter came in to work the next day and magically found himself greeted as "Mr. Vice President." He had a security clearance, a secretary, a support staff, and a corner office on one of the highest floors of the building. It was exactly as Milton had promised. Thus began a meteoric rise as Walter requested and Milton granted one wish after another until Walter was President and CEO of the largest corporation in the world. Everyone looked up to Walter and he was very, very happy. He often said to himself, "I am Walter, and I am on top of the world. No one is bigger or more important than I am."

But then one day Walter heard footsteps, strangely, in the rooftop garden of his penthouse office. He went outside and found a small boy on his knees praying.

"Are you praying to Walter, to me?" Walter asked.

The little boy answered, "Of course not! I don't even know who you are. I am praying to Jesus."

Walter was deeply disturbed by this. He thought he was at the very top of everything. How could someone, even Jesus, be more important than Walter? So after a fitful night of no sleep, he demanded that Milton, that magical, talking cockroach be brought before him once again. Milton quickly appeared.

"I have one last wish, Milton," Walter said, "and upon granting this wish I set you free for there will be nothing left to ask. I wish to be like Jesus."

Milton said, "As you wish."

The next day when Walter came to work he was back in the mailroom.

Get small. Be vulnerable. Humble yourself. Let go of your rights and what you think you deserve. Be a slave. Be a child. This is what it means to follow Jesus, to be like Jesus and to enter the kingdom of God. We spend most of our lives, even after we come to faith, protecting our honor, defending our place in the world and scraping to get to the top of the heap. It's one grand adventure in missing the point.

Children don't live that way. Children live their lives with simplicity, not having acquired the mindset of harming others to gain some level of self-imposed success. A child—whether seven or seventy—is that person who still has a trusting heart, who is still dependent upon the Father and who has not lost the God-given gift of humility. It is one who is still small and seemingly insignificant. That is the essence of what it means to be a *talya*—a slave, a child, a little one—one willing to "happily accept the cookies," as Brennan Manning said, "that is the kingdom of God."25

The pressing question then is how? How do we put this into practice? Frankly, we simply put it into practice! When someone steps on us on their way to the top, we pray for the grace not to grab them by the ankle so that they fall. When our rights get violated (and they will), we seek the mind of Christ that empowers us to let these offenses go. When someone, something, or some circumstance is standing in the way of our success, and we want to prove we can crush all obstacles with our Herculean abilities and our gigantic egos, we go to the nursery and sit with a child until the desire fades. When we sense that we are headed down the path that leads us away from childlike simplicity and dependence upon God, we stop dead in our tracks and remember that there can be no striving in the kingdom of God. Spiritually, figuratively, emotionally—physically and literally if we must—we resist and get away from those things that lure us into a state where we are not wholly and completely dependent upon God.

The essence of a child, the crux of what it means to be a slave, is humble dependence with no thought given to personal status or prominence. Children and slaves—*talyas*—do not set the agendas of their households. They are not capable of creating their own way. They don't make things happen. They don't exert authority or make demands. They simply receive what is given to them with humility, and they enter the world with the inverted power of humble, vulnerable service to others.

The objections are obvious: if we do this, it will put us at a disadvantage in the world. It will make us susceptible. We might get taken advantage of. We might not succeed. People won't see what we are actually capable of doing. We might be stepped on or disrespected.

If these objections are your thoughts, your assessment is correct on all counts, but you are also on the way to getting it! No, the world doesn't operate this way, but this is exactly why the witness of the church is required. In a society marked by smear campaigns, scrapping and fighting to prevail, grotesque levels of inequality and greed, broken promises and broken deals, cheating and killing just to get to the top of the heap, when we become as children or servants, we show the world a better way to live. We demonstrate that the most radical and world-changing thing we can do is "stop believing in the dominant systems and rules of this world," and live lives that are "contradictions full of hope and promise."26 This is far more than a witness, however; it is also how Jesus himself lived.

The Apostle Paul, with some of his best and highest words, described the example of Jesus in Philippians 2. Paul writes: "Don't be selfish; don't try to impress others. Be humble, thinking of others as better than yourselves. Don't look out only for your own interests, but take an interest in others, too. You must have the same attitude that Christ Jesus had" (verses 3–5). And what is the attitude of Jesus? Paul answers, "He [Jesus] gave up his divine privileges and he took the humble position of a slave" (verse 7).

Of course, if you start thinking about Jesus, the Son of God, emptying himself and giving up his "divine privileges," it can warp your mind. How could this happen? How could God empty himself like that? It is a beautiful mystery. It is one worth thinking and meditating on, how the essence and infinity of God could be crammed into the limitations of a human being. But if all we do is sit and think about it (or compose theological doctrines about it), all we will end up with is a headache. Paul's intent in writing these words was not to provide a full explanation for the life of Jesus. He was not writing a doctrinal treatise or telling us what to believe. He wrote this to provide an example of how to live our lives like Jesus. It is the life of love and humble service—whatever the cost—even death on a cross.

This is what Jesus taught, what Jesus lived, and we must live it too! If we refuse to live it, then nothing else we do will matter, because nothing more or less than this will do.

Thankfully, from time to time, God has gifted the church with those rare individuals who remind us of Jesus' words and our proper identities that are as small as a child and as humble as a servant. One of those people was a French teenager who lived a century ago named Thérèse Martin, better known today as St. Thérèse of Lisieux. Thérèse entered a Carmelite convent when she was only a teenager, following in the steps of her two older sisters. Raised in a devoted and pious family, she had but one ambition: to become a saint. The Carmelites certainly lent themselves to her pursuit.

It was the Carmelite Order that had produced John of the Cross and Teresa of Avila, believers who were eventually sainted for their profound devotion and spiritual insights. Further, the Carmelites demanded strict obedience, continuous prayers, long periods of fasting and silence, vows of isolation and poverty, and a severe approach to spirituality. This was the perfect place for one looking to achieve the peak of the religious honor system. And this was the exact place that Thérèse utterly failed.

Six years into her cloistered life in the convent, and suffering from poor health and debilitating bouts of depression, she realized that all her striving and religious go-getting was useless. She was exhausted by it all and simply could not do it. Giving up on sainthood altogether, and despairing of life, it was about this time that she read a simple line from the book of Proverbs that changed everything: *si quis est parvulus veniat ad me*. "Whoso is little, let him come to me." She named this discovery "Petite Voie," or "The Little Way," and realized that the only way up was down.

For the rest of her very short life (she died in her mid-twenties), she quit trying so hard at trying so hard and learned to become a child again. She wrote, "Children are always giving trouble, falling down, getting themselves dirty, breaking things; but all this does not shake their parents' love for them,"27 and, "So there is no need for me to grow up. I must stay little and become less and less. I rejoice to be little because only children, and those who are like them, will be admitted to the heavenly banquet."28

Often critiqued as overly simplistic and naïve, Thérèse and her "Little Way" are rejected by those who feel the need for greater complexity or intellectualism in their faith. Maybe these critics reject her conclusions because they simply feel the need for more: more responsibility, more steps up the religious ladder to the top, more ways to gain respect, status, or a higher standing, and the need for a more honorable reputation. Yet, it appears that Thérèse was right on target, and not because her way ironically led to her sainthood. She was right because her way reflected the way of Jesus. And reflecting Jesus is more than enough, because his way, "The Little Way," always leads us to abandon ourselves like a child, into the arms of God.

Chapter 5

Put Out the Fire

At that point Peter got up the nerve to ask, "Master, how many times do I forgive a brother or sister who hurts me? Seven?" Jesus replied, "Seven! Hardly. Try seventy times seven. The kingdom of God is like a king who decided to square accounts with his servants. As he got under way, one servant was brought before him who had run up a debt of a hundred thousand dollars. He couldn't pay up, so the king ordered the man, along with his wife, children, and goods, to be auctioned off at the slave market. The poor wretch threw himself at the king's feet and begged, 'Give me a chance and I'll pay it all back.' Touched by his plea, the king let him off, erasing the debt. The servant was no sooner out of the room when he came upon one of his fellow servants who owed him ten dollars. He seized him by the throat and demanded, 'Pay up. Now!' The poor wretch threw himself down and begged, 'Give me a chance and I'll pay it all back.' But he wouldn't do it. He had him arrested and put in jail until the debt was paid. When the other servants saw this going on, they were outraged and brought a detailed report to the king. The king summoned the man and said, 'You evil servant! I forgave your entire debt when you begged me for mercy. Shouldn't you be compelled to be merciful to your fellow servant who asked for mercy?'"

—MATTHEW 18:21–33 (THE MESSAGE)

LAL SHAHBAZ QALANDAR WAS a holy man and scholar born in the 1100s whose ancient travels sound as contemporary as today's news feeds. He was born in what is now Afghanistan; he was the descendant of immigrating Iraqis; he lived and died in Pakistan; and his shrine was constructed by donations from the Iranian royalty. Maybe the only thing more extraordinary than Lal Shahbaz's wide-reaching travels are the many mythological stories that have been attached to him over the centuries.

In one such story Lal Shahbaz was wandering through the desert with a friend as evening began to fall. The desert was terribly cold, so the two pilgrims began to gather wood for a fire. With their pyre neatly constructed, they realized that they had no way of igniting it. Lal Shahbaz's friend suggested that he transform himself into a great bird (the meaning of "Shahbaz") and fly down into hell to collect coals for a fire. Lal Shahbaz considered this a wise suggestion and flew away. After many cold hours Lal Shahbaz returned to his friend empty-handed. Puzzled, he asked why he had not returned with fire to keep them warm. Lal Shahbaz replied, "There is no fire in hell. Everyone who goes there brings their own fire and their own pain, from this world."29

There is a great deal of truth in this old story. If we think of hell as a self-imposed prison or a self-ignited blaze, then Lal Shahbaz is correct: Anyone suffering from the results of their own hard-hearted decisions or their own hand is truly suffering hell. They have not been cast away by God; they have kindled their own fire. They have hurt themselves, and nothing hurts worse than self-inflicted wounds.

By Jesus' definition, the most "burning torture to bear"30 is the scorching heat of resentment and unforgiveness. As a postscript to the Lord's Prayer he instructed, "If you forgive those who sin against you, your heavenly Father will forgive you. But if you refuse to forgive others, your Father will not forgive your sins" (Matthew 6:14–15). When we refuse to forgive others, we sentence ourselves and our world to hellish suffering. When we choose to carry our own fire and our own pain with us through life, we abandon God's heavenly reign on earth. Our participation in the mission of Christ—our very communion with the Father—depends upon our willingness to extinguish the burning inferno in our souls by forgiving those who have harmed us.

The clearest example of this kind of forgiveness in all of Jesus' teachings is found in a story unique to Matthew's Gospel. In Matthew 18:21–35, we encounter a tale traditionally referred to as "The Parable of the Unmerciful Servant," another of those parables that Jesus uses to describe the kingdom of God. It is a simple, direct story, which Jesus concludes by saying, "That's what my heavenly Father will do to you if you refuse to forgive your brothers and sisters from your heart," (verse 35) that I will summarize here:

A king, who had lent money to his servants, called in his debts. One loan was to a servant who owed 10,000 talents. A talent was a denomination of money. If these were talents of gold, then this loan was in the neighborhood, by today's standards, of $3 billion; an obscene amount of money. But, it may have been even more than that, as 10,000 talents was more money than was in circulation in all of Palestine in the first century.31 Had Jesus been telling this story in the United States today, this would be a debt exceeding a trillion dollars.

This man owed the world, and the king prepared to take everything from him, sell the debtor's family into slavery, and throw the man into prison. The debtor begged for mercy and promised to pay the debt back (an absolute impossibility given the amount). The king was so moved by the appeal of his servant that he forgave the entire debt. He didn't give the man an extension or restructure this bad loan. He didn't reduce the interest rate or the principle. The king executed a complete and total bailout.

As the newly forgiven debtor left the king's palace, literally just outside the door, he met one of his own debtors. This man owed him about $1,000. The unmerciful servant grabbed him by the throat and demanded immediate payment. Word for word, this thousand-dollar debtor begged for more time to pay his debt, but the man who had just been released from a $1 trillion liability, threw the man who owed him $1,000 into debtor's prison. Of course, word got back to the king who reacted with justifiable rage.

He called the man back in and said, "I forgave you that tremendous debt because you pleaded with me. Shouldn't you have mercy on your fellow servant, just as I had mercy on you" (Matthew 18:32-33 NLT)? Then the king sent the man to prison until he had paid his entire debt. Jesus concluded the story by saying, "That's what my heavenly Father will do to you if you refuse to forgive your brothers and sisters from your heart" Matthew 18:35, NLT).

Jesus does not tell this story in a vacuum. Earlier in Matthew 18, Jesus had discussed different aspects of reconciliation. This produced an impulsive question from Simon Peter and the occasion for this parable. Peter asked, "Lord, how often should I forgive someone who sins against me? Seven times?" (verse 21). The rabbis of Jesus' day taught a "three-strikes-and-you're-out" rule of forgiveness (based loosely on an interpretation of Amos 1:3—2:16). On the fourth offense, the sinner was on his or her own. "Why should human beings be more gracious or do better than God?" the logic went. So when Peter proposed a seven-fold forgiveness, he was doubling the usual expectation and adding one more for good measure. Peter had to feel pretty good about his answer, for it was very generous.

Yet, in the always upside down way of Jesus, the Lord answers, "No, not seven times, but seventy times seven!" (Matthew 18:22). Technically, that's 490 instances of forgiveness, but technicality is not Jesus' apparent point. Jesus was instructing his disciples to stop keeping score. "Always forgive," was his answer. There should be no limitation attached to the number of times the disciples of Jesus forgive others.

Now, the inescapable question: how could Jesus say such a thing? It is utterly ridiculous. Forgive every time? I can understand turning the other cheek until you run out of cheeks. I can understand walking the second mile. I even get it when he says things like, "Do good to those who persecute you." But to forgive every single time you are hurt, harmed, offended, cheated on, ripped off, mistreated, abused, molested, raped, battered, fired, wrongly accused, or verbally assaulted—every time—this is lunacy!

Here's the answer: when we forgive others without limit, we are treating others as God treats us and how he treats the world. When we react with grace, we are reacting as God reacts.

Throughout all of human history, from the first murder just steps outside the garden of Eden to the Holocaust of the Jews, from the first emergence of the warring tribes in the Middle East to the genocide now occurring in Darfur, God continues to let the earth spin on its axis, and he allows the universe to continue to hum along. He hasn't snuffed it out or thrown it away. He hasn't given up on it. He hasn't given up on us. Why? Because he is not willing that any should perish, but that all should come to redemption and salvation.

"I will forgive you up to a point, but then I will never forgive you again," is simply not something God can say to humanity. God loves and God forgives and he does so without restraint or limitation. So when Jesus teaches us to forgive without limit, he is simply calling us to mirror and to reflect the love and grace of heaven on earth. He is calling us to live up to our creative purpose—to properly bear the loving image of God in the world. We forgive without limit because that's what God does.

This raises another inescapable question: is God-like forgiveness humanly possible? Yes, if it remains God's work! Forgiveness is not something we can accomplish on our own or within our own power (no more than we make the kingdom of God happen in the world). It's not something we conjure up. If forgiveness flows out of us to others, it is because God is doing it and not us ourselves.

Consider those words we have prayed countless times: "Forgive us our trespasses, as we forgive those who trespass against us" (Matthew 6:12 KJV). This phrase could be accurately translated: "Empower us to forgive others, with the forgiveness you have given us." In praying that prayer, we admit and acknowledge that our ability to forgive comes from God. It is rooted in his forgiveness and grace. God must do it for us and through us, or it cannot be done.

Thus, the grace that God has given to us is both the motivation and the method for granting grace to our own offenders. Because we have received God's personal forgiveness, we have both the "why" and the "way" to personally forgive others. Pardon *received* from heaven becomes pardon *relayed* on earth. And anywhere we see forgiveness playing itself out—between husband and wife, parent and child, black and white, Arab and Jew—wherever—we are seeing God at work. We are bearing witness to the fierce, supernatural mercy of heaven being manifested on earth.

Witnessing this type of forgiveness may be the only adequate way to actually describe it, and this may be the reason that Jesus responded to Peter's question about forgiveness with a story rather than a lecture. Jesus wanted the disciples to "see" it, not hear about it. In that regard, describing forgiveness is a bit like Supreme Court Justice Potter Stewart describing pornography. He quipped, "I could never succeed in defining it, but I know it when I see it."[32] To understand forgiveness, we must see or experience it, and when we do, we come to know that something supernatural has taken place.

One of the first ways I "saw" and came to understand forgiveness was in a woman much beloved by my Sunday School teachers, a woman named Corrie Ten Boom. I heard Ten Boom's story so often and told with such holy reverence that at times I was sure she was in the Bible, tucked away somewhere in the Old Testament. She certainly would have been one the biblical writers could not have ignored.

Corrie Ten Boom and her family were Dutch Christians who sheltered Jews in their home during the Second World War. People were always hiding behind the false walls and floors of their house, and Corrie's memoir, *The Hiding Place*, records those events.[33] That book also records their betrayal into the hands of the Nazis. The Ten Booms were arrested and scattered across different concentration camps all over Europe. Corrie and her sister Betsie were sent to Ravensbruck, and by the end of the war, all the Ten Booms had died while incarcerated except for Corrie. Corrie gained notoriety in the years that followed as she traveled and shared her experiences. These travels pushed her even deeper into God's forgiveness as evidenced by her own account from 1947:

> I had come from Holland to defeated Germany with the message that God forgives. It was in a church in Munich that I saw him, a balding heavy-set man in a gray overcoat, a brown felt hat clutched between his hands. People

were filing out of the basement room where I had just spoken. . . . This man had been a guard at Ravensbruck concentration camp. He came up to me and said, "You mentioned Ravensbruck in your talk. I was a guard there." He did not remember me. "But since that time I have become a Christian. I know that God has forgiven me for the cruel things I did there, but I would like to hear it from your lips as well. Fraulein," his hand came out, "will you forgive me?"

I stood there—and could not. Betsie had died in that place—could he erase her slow terrible death simply for the asking? While only seconds, it seemed like hours passed as I wrestled with the most difficult thing I had ever had to do . . . the coldness clutching my heart. "Jesus, help me!" I prayed silently. "I can lift my hand, I can do that much." And so woodenly, mechanically, I thrust my hand into the one stretched out to me. And as I did, an incredible thing took place. . . . This healing warmth seemed to flood my whole being, bringing tears to my eyes.

"I forgive you, my brother!" I cried, "with all my heart!" For a long moment we grasped each other's hands, the former guard and the former prisoner. I had never known God's love so intensely as I did then.34

Forgiveness does not ignore the terrible transgressions committed against us. Unfaithfulness by a spouse, betrayal by a business partner, abuse by a parent, mistreatment by a priest or pastor, the drunk driver who harmed or killed one of our family members: the offense and hurt we feel is legitimate, and we must confess that wrongdoing is, indeed, wrong. But rather than responding to these wrongs with the hellfire of revenge or resentment, we respond with compassion and grace, a grace that comes from God.

Our only responsibility in this process is to be a conduit, a passage through which God's forgiveness can flow, and a reflective mirror of God's own love to us. We simply extend an empty hand—woodenly and mechanically if necessary—and pray, "Jesus, help me!" And help he will. As he draws near, he will bring a profound realization and understanding of God's love, and the better we understand God's love, the more that love will spill out to others. Consequently, forgiveness is not so much something we do, as it is something we discover.35 It is the discovery of God's inexhaustible, inconceivable, insuppressible love—for ourselves—and even for those who have hurt us.

An example: there is a television show on the A&E Network called "Storage Wars." Storage units that have been abandoned or defaulted upon by the renters are opened, and bidders show up to bid competitively for the contents of the unit. Sometimes bidders lose their shirt, and sometimes they make a little money. An anonymous man in San Jose did a bit better than that recently. He bought the contents of a storage unit from Dan and Laura Dotson, the hosts of "Storage Wars," for one thousand one hundred dollars. This particular unit belonged to an elderly woman who had passed away, and none of her survivors had assumed the monthly payment. When the payments lapsed, the storage facility was turned over to the Dotsons to handle the sale of the items left inside. At auction the San Jose man made his bid of one thousand one hundred dollars, a bit high, but he was motivated by all the plastic storage boxes, "because whatever was inside was probably worth more than what's inside cardboard boxes," he said. He was right. Inside one of those plastic boxes were nearly two thousand gold and silver Spanish coins—literally a pirate's treasure trove—worth more than five hundred thousand dollars.36

Forgiveness, I think, works like that: we begin sorting through the baggage and the storage units of our lives. We start unpacking our pain and injustice, rummaging through it all, betting and hoping for something worth keeping. While we busily sort, shuffle, and restack the boxes of our past hurts, lo and behold, we stumble across a treasure. We didn't earn it. We didn't work for it. We didn't manufacture it. Simply, there it is, and it was there all along, right in the midst of all our rubbish: the unexpected, glorious discovery of God's unlimited grace. He really loves us, and his love becomes large enough within us that we can forgive those who have hurt us. It is this discovery of forgiveness that can change us and change the world.

Do I really believe that forgiveness can change the world? Well, if it can't, then we are out of business. What was the crux of Jesus' teachings? What was his life about? What was the meaning of the cross? How has the church endured for all of these centuries? If it's not about the transforming love and forgiveness of God for both the individual and the world, what are we doing here? Isn't the most beloved verse of the New Testament still "For God loved the world so much that he gave his one and only Son, so that everyone who believes in him will not perish but have eternal life" (John 3:16)? God's forgiveness will change the world—it must—for it is the only thing that has ever really worked to truly absolve and resolve the past. It is the only thing that closes the door on what happened yesterday and opens the door to a better future.

Dr. Fred Luskin says it like this: "To forgive is to give up all hope for a better past. . . . Forgiveness allows you a fresh start. . . . It's like a rain coming to a polluted environment. It clears things. At some point, you can say that this awful thing happened to me. It hurt like hell, yet I'm not going to allow it to take over my life."37 If we don't believe that, if we do not believe that forgiveness can in fact change the world and give the world a future, then as clearly as I know how to say it, we do not believe the gospel. Forgiveness has given us a future, and it can do the same for everyone else. Forgiveness can overcome the worst atrocities and put out the fire of our collective pain.

So when the wounds and scars of our world are paraded out as means and motivation for further hate and revenge, we must counter that there is no future in the vicious cycles of unforgiveness and retaliation. When we hear the names of Auschwitz, Treblinka, and Ravensbruck, we answer with the names of Maximilian Kolbe, Corrie Ten Boom, and Bernard Lichtenberg—people who were not overcome by evil, but overcame evil with good. When someone speaks of the hate and injustice in South Africa, we speak the names of Nelson Mandela and Desmond Tutu who continue to heal a nation. When we hear of the past and current atrocities in Darfur, Armenia, Syria, Sandy Hook, Selma, or Croatia, we answer with the names of Martin Luther King Jr., Mother Teresa, Miroslav Volf,

Dirk Willems, the Amish of Nickel Mines, and Yitzhak Rabin who lived, suffered, and died for the sake of forgiveness.

And I'll add one more name to this list: Amy Biehl.

In the summer of 1993, white rule was ending in South Africa. As the first free elections were about to take place, the country descended into violence. White fundamentalists attempted to hold to power, and disenfranchised young blacks rioted in the streets. On an August night, a mob of angry young men was looking for symbols of white rule to destroy. That's when they spotted Amy Biehl as she drove through the township, and they succeeded in stopping her car. She ran for her life but was chased down by the mob, stoned, and stabbed to death. Amy Biehl was not their enemy, however. She had been in Cape Town for a year, a Stanford graduate and Fulbright scholar studying and working to end apartheid. She had a plane ticket in her car to fly home to California the next day.

Four members of the mob were charged and convicted of murder. The prosecution asked for the death penalty, but the judge sentenced them to eighteen years in prison, saying he thought that they had a chance to become useful citizens. Four years later, these four men applied for a pardon before the nation's Truth and Reconciliation Commission. At the hearing, the men admitted their role in Amy's killing and said that they believed they had to kill whites to force the government to relinquish power. They each received a pardon and were set free. More remarkably, they received a pardon from Amy's parents and family.

Two of the men who killed Amy Biehl, in fact, now work for the charity that Biehl's parents founded after she was killed. The Amy Biehl Foundation is an international non-profit in Cape Town that runs children's programs, a bakery, sponsors welding classes and after-school programs, teaches music and art, and readies young South Africans to go to college. Ntobeko Peni is the program manager, and Easy Nofemela is the Sports Director—both men were in the mob on that August night that ended Amy Biehl's life.

Ntobeko says, "Deep down, it was very difficult for me to accept my own actions, but when I think of Amy. . . . One has to find peace within in order to live. This foundation helped me forgive myself."38

The only way to stop the continual and rampant hate in this world is to make peace. The only way to make peace is to forgive. The only way to forgive is through the unrelenting love and forgiveness of God. We are the instruments of that peace. We are the tools of God's forgiveness. We are the images of God's love. That love will extinguish the fires of hell. That love will indeed bring reconciliation to the world, and if reconciliation isn't heaven come to earth, then nothing is.

Chapter 6

Bleeding Charity

Peter said to Jesus, "We've given up everything to follow you. What will we get?" Jesus replied, "Everyone who has given up houses or brothers or sisters or father or mother or children or property, for my sake, will receive a hundred times as much in return and will inherit eternal life. But many who are the greatest now will be least important then, and those who seem least important now will be the greatest then. ... For the Kingdom of Heaven is like the landowner who went out early one morning to hire workers for his vineyard. He agreed to pay the normal daily wage and sent them out to work. At nine o'clock in the morning he was passing through the marketplace and saw some people standing around doing nothing. So he hired them, telling them he would pay them whatever was right at the end of the day. So they went to work in the vineyard. At noon and again at three o'clock he did the same thing. At five o'clock that afternoon he was in town again and saw some more people standing around. He asked them, 'Why haven't you been working today?' They replied, 'Because no one hired us.' The landowner told them, 'Then go out and join the others in my vineyard.' That evening he told the foreman to call the workers in and pay them, beginning with the last workers first. When those hired at five o'clock were paid, each received a full day's wage. When those hired first came to get their pay, they assumed they would receive more. But they, too, were paid a day's wage. When they received their pay, they protested to the owner, 'Those people worked only one hour, and yet you've paid them just as much as you paid us who worked all day in the scorching heat.' He answered one of them, 'Friend, I haven't been unfair! Didn't you agree to work all day for the usual wage? Take your money and go. I wanted to pay this last worker the same as you. Is it against the law for me to do what I want with my money? Should you be jealous because I am kind to others?' So those who are last now will be first then, and those who are first will be last."

—MATTHEW 19:27, 29—20:16 (NLT)

It all began harmlessly enough. I was sitting at dinner with my family when my wife declared that she would be participating in an upcoming 5K charity run. She turned to our three boys and said, "You should run with me!" They are athletic and competitive, so all three thought this was a wonderful challenge. Seeing their enthusiasm, and feeling a bit like I was on the outside looking in, I casually said, "That would be fun. I could even run with you." In orchestrated unison, they all broke into hysterical laughter.

Clearly I deserved this type of reaction. I've always said to my family and my jogging-sprinting-marathoning friends, that if they ever see me running along the side of the road, they should stop and help me; something or someone terrible is obviously chasing me. I just don't enjoy it. It seems a waste of time and energy, and frankly, the act of running any real distance just plain hurts my body. Still, the condescension from my wife and children wounded me deeply, and like any man in midlife with wounded pride, my ego was stronger than my pain. So, then and there, with the chuckles around the dinner table still hanging in the air, I decided that I would indeed run the upcoming race, and I would be the one with the last laugh.

Not losing a moment, and knowing that the preparation window was quickly closing, I started readying myself the very next day. I downloaded one of those training regimens that transforms a couch potato like me into a competitor in just a matter of a few weeks. It consisted of walking a little bit, and then jogging a little bit. The next week I would walk further and jog further, increasing the pace and the distance. On and on this went until race day when I gathered with five thousand new friends at the starting line and off we went in multi-colored, spandex-clad wonder.

I didn't set any land speed records with my first ever 5K run. In fact, I finished a full twenty minutes behind the young man who won the race, but I didn't care. I finished, and that is all that mattered to me. And all those laughing, disparaging chumps around the dinner table that night? Where were they when I crossed the finish line? They had all opted for the one-mile "Family Fun Run" and never even entered the race. Maybe it was a trick all along. But trick or not, I finished, and even if I had been the last one across the finish line, I would have celebrated like I had just set a world record.

Here in Matthew 20 is a kingdom story about those who finish last, yet they are treated as if they had finished first. Trophies, ribbons, and prize money are handed out to the losers, and for some in the story (and for those of us who now hear these words of Jesus), it sounds as if there is some kind of trick involved. Jesus turns apparent fairness and equity on their ear.

The occasion for this story is a question posed squarely by Simon Peter. He was always good at being direct, and whether it was bravery or absurdity, he often articulated what others were thinking but were afraid to ask. His question: "What's in it for me?" The disciples had given up everything to follow Jesus, and they were the first to do so. When the whistle sounded to begin the work that is the kingdom of God in this world, they were the first ones on the job. They wanted to know what they would get for their trailblazing hard work and dedication. Jesus answers with this parable, a parable about a vineyard, a landowner and a day's wage for less than a day's work. This parable doesn't answer Simon Peter's question as much as it points all disciples to a broader view of God's grace.

In first-century Palestine, vineyards were common. Thus, when the time of the grape harvest arrived, entire communities would mobilize to get those grapes to the winery. Landowners and vineyard managers, pressed by the demands of the now-ready fruit, would daily visit the local marketplace to find willing workers. The marketplace was where all the vendors, salespeople, and tradesmen plied their wares, and it is where the unemployed and day laborers gathered for the chance to get a little work. This is exactly the scene Jesus describes in this parable.

A variation of this exercise plays itself out in a community in which I once lived, the city of Ellijay, Georgia, the "Apple Capital" of the Southeastern United States. Grown in these Appalachian orchards are Matsus, Granny Smiths, Winesaps, Roman Beauties, Fujitas, Pink Ladies, and about a dozen more varieties of apple. For all their diversity of taste and color, they all have one thing in common: a short harvest season. Beginning in early August and extending until Thanksgiving or so (depending upon the weather), the apples from all the orchards have to be harvested or they will be lost.

The owners of the orchards are forced by the harvest to find as many workers as possible. They hire cousins, neighbors, in-laws, stepbrothers, and the teenagers they fired for poor performance the previous season. They advertise for seasonal workers, beg, search, borrow, recruit, and steal every able-bodied soul they can find as unemployment in the community shrinks to nothing. The rush of the harvest requires drastic measures to get the crop out of the orchards and to the market.

This is the exact situation that Jesus describes for his disciples: "The kingdom of God is like the landowner who went out early one morning to hire workers for his vineyard." There is an eagerness to bring as many workers as possible into the field. Some will work all day. Others will give most of the day, others part of the day, and some will arrive at the eleventh hour. There's more than enough work to do, and there is more than enough reward to go around. It is that reward—the goodness of the landowners toward his workers—that frustrates what would be an otherwise simple story.

The landowner, inexplicably, pays those who were hired last and worked the least the same wage as those who were hired first and worked all day long. No matter which way you cut it, this doesn't seem very fair, especially for those of us raised with entrepreneurial capitalism in our blood, and with a sense that "membership has its privileges," membership we have duly earned. This is completely unacceptable, and it was for some of those in Jesus' story.

Imagine the scene as it plays out. The work day is over. The tired workers line up for their pay and the landowner asks that those hired last be paid first. He gives them all a full day's wage. Meanwhile, those who were hired first see this and begin to chat excitedly among themselves. "Those who worked only an hour got a full day's pay! Just imagine what we are going to get!" So when the Director of Human Resources gets to them with their checks, these are for the same amount as those who worked only an hour.

Quickly, there is the threat of a labor riot. The union representative gets called to the work site, and workers begin filing suits for unfair labor practices. Word gets back to the landowner, so he returns to the vineyard with a response to one of the disgruntled workers: "Friend, I haven't been unfair! Didn't you agree to work all day for the usual wage? Take your money and go. I wanted to pay this last worker the same as you. Is it against the law for me to do what I want with my money? Should you be jealous because I am kind to others?"

It is a direct and forceful response, but it is also so very kind. First, he calls those who protest his "friends." He has no grumble with them and is grateful for all they have done. Second, he points out that he has been very fair to them, paying them exactly as their contract stipulated. Finally—*and this is the punch line to the entire story*—he says, in effect, "My generosity is mine to do with as I please. You are not angry because I have been unfair. You are angry *because I have been generous and gracious to others.*"

The landowner understood that unemployment for an itinerant worker, unemployment for just a single day, would sentence the worker and his family to a fitful night of hunger and growling stomachs. If the worker didn't work, neither he nor his family would eat. The owner understood this desperation and the very real need of the workers, even those who had arrived late in the day. Thus, the landowner gave the late-arriving laborers not what they had earned, but what they actually needed. The landowner gave grace, and this is what infuriated the other workers.

With this story, Jesus has dug his fingers into an extremely sore spot for we who are religious people. We preach grace, but we don't always practice it. We talk about God's mercy, but we don't always want the people who need it most to know it or get in on it. We say we are in the redemption business, but the door to that redemption is often locked by us from the inside. We say, "Come in! All are welcome!" but "all" is often marked with an asterisk. How, I ask, can the world change—how can heaven come to earth—if we stingily protest against God for his grace to others, grace we have freely received ourselves? How can we pray "thy kingdom come," and be resentful toward God and those he allows to enter the kingdom in his way and his timing?

There's an old joke about a man arriving at the gates of heaven. St. Peter asks, "What is your denomination?" The man says, "Methodist." St. Peter looks down his list and says, "Okay, go to room twenty-four, but be very quiet as you pass room eight." Another man arrives at the gates of heaven. St. Peter asks, "What is your denomination?" The man answers, "Catholic." St. Peter looks at his list again and says, "Very well, go to room eighteen, but be very quiet as you pass room eight." A third man arrives at the gates. A third time Peter asks, "What is your denomination?" The man says, "Baptist." He checks the manifest a third time and says, "Go to room eleven but be very quiet as you pass room eight." The man says, "I can understand there being different rooms for different religions and different denominations, but why must I be quiet when I pass room eight?" St. Peter tells him, "Well, the Presbyterians are in room eight, and they think they are the only ones here."

Such real attitudes prevail today, not just in a hypothetical eternity, and these attitudes are a severe detriment to God's witness in the world. So here is an exercise for you. Suppose you get to heaven and there inside the pearly gates are Mother Theresa, C.S. Lewis, your sweet grandmother, Martin Luther, your childhood dog, St. Patrick, the twelve disciples, the old pastor that first pointed you to faith—all the usual and expected people you would imagine to find there. But walking with them to meet you is Adolf Hitler, and he is singing the songs of the saints and praising the name of Christ. With him is Osama bin Laden, a converted follower of Christ who slipped in at the last minute. What about Jeffery Dahmer, Jerry Sandusky, Ted Bundy, Genghis Khan, Timothy McVeigh, Wayne Williams, Saddam Hussein, or a thousand other vile and despicable people? What if they were all there? Would you walk in, look around, and protest to God? Would you ask for a refund? Would you file suit in the heavenly court and complain about God's generosity and grace, or would you just be glad that we were all there together?

My friend Landon Saunders says that "figuring out who is in and who is out is just too much work. It's too heavy of a burden! So I just try to treat every person I meet as if they will be sitting beside me at the table in eternity." Such a small change of perspective would do more to advance the kingdom of God on earth than a thousand aggrieved churches that pound their pulpits and their parishioners with unyielding dogma, point fingers, condemn and exclude others from the love of God.

To that end, there is a delightful little book, a personal favorite of mine, written by C.S. Lewis entitled *The Great Divorce*.39 It's not a huge epic like his Narnia collection, or a classic in the same way as *Mere Christianity*. It's less than one hundred fifty pages, but it is dynamite, an allegory somewhere between *Pilgrim's Progress* and Dante's *Inferno* where the narrator of the story (who is having an incredible, vivid dream) finds himself living in a dark, gray, colorless, and joyless town that turns out to be some kind of hell or purgatory. But there is this bus that leaves the town on a regular basis, taking those who choose to visit a faraway place that turns out to be the foothills of heaven. So the plot circulates around these travelers on this bus who arrive in the most beautiful heaven conceivable, but they are overwhelmed by the experience.

The glorious light burns their skin and eyes, and they are reduced to shadowy ghosts. The grass beneath their feet feels like they are walking on needles. The water from the beautiful streams runs over them like sandpaper. A leaf or a tree branch feels like it weighs thousands of pounds. If a raindrop in this heaven were to strike them on the head it would land like a concrete block. And the distance from where they first arrive to the expansive mountains and the heavenly city on the far away horizon is infinitely too far to travel. The people of earth are simply unfit for heaven.

Men and women they have known on earth—but who are now wonderfully transformed with rippling muscles, shining countenances, and the most beautiful, happy eyes and faces—come out to meet the people from the gray city. They offer their counsel and assistance to help these new arrivals on the journey toward the mountains and the higher elevations of heaven. The task put before the shadow people is to decide whether or not they will stay in heaven and "work out their own salvation," or get back on the bus and return to the gray, hopeless town. Most of them return because they can't—or won't—let go of the things that have kept them bound in hell.

In an early scene in the book a man gets off the bus and recognizes immediately that he has finally arrived in some type of heaven. While he is still wondering what it is all about, he is met by an old employee of his—one of the shining people—whose name is Les. The man is dumbfounded to see Les so youthful, bright, and transformed. More so, he is surprised to see Les at all, in heaven of all places, for Les was a violent, murderous man!

He says, "This isn't right, Les . . . you murdered Jack. What about poor Jack?"

And Les answered, "Of course I murdered him. But it is all right now. Jack is here. You will meet him soon, if you will stay. He sends you his love."

The man from earth can't stand it. He screams back, "What I'd like to understand is what you are doing here, as pleased as punch you bloody murderer, while I've been walking the streets down there and living in a place like a pig sty all these years."

The man blusters and argues defending his goodness and morality while attacking Les for his failures and murdering their friend, Jack. He begins to end his argument by saying, "I only want my rights. I'm not asking for anybody's bleeding charity."

Then in a stroke of gospel genius, C.S. Lewis puts these words in Les' mouth as he responds: "Then do. At once. Ask for the Bleeding Charity. Everything is here for the asking and nothing can be bought. . . . Murdering old Jack wasn't the worst thing I did. . . . I murdered you in my heart for years. . . . That is why I have been sent to you now: to ask your forgiveness and to be your servant as long as you need one, longer if it pleases you."

The poor man from the gray town could now take no more. He says, "I'm not making pals with a murderer, let alone taking lessons from him. . . . Tell them I'm not coming. I'd rather be damned than go along with you. I came here to get my rights, you see? Not to go sniveling along on charity tied onto your apron-strings. . . . I'll go home. That's what I'll do." The narrator concludes: "And in the end, still grumbling, but whimpering also a little as he picked his way over the sharp grasses, he made off back to the bus."40

The kingdom of God is not about fairness. It's not about justice or earning what is rightfully yours. It's not about what's in it for you. The kingdom of God is only for the asking. It is about grace. And if we get there at sunrise or just before the sun slips over the horizon; if we come to faith while still wearing diapers or wrapped in the covers of our deathbed; if we were diligent and hardworking or stumbled into the vineyard having overslept and wasted most of the day, we all make it in the same way: by the grace of God, the "Bleeding Charity" that is the love of Jesus.

Chapter 7

Where Nothing Is Sacred

A man sitting at the table with Jesus exclaimed, "What a blessing it will be to attend a banquet in the Kingdom of God!" Jesus replied with this story: "A man prepared a great feast and sent out many invitations. When the banquet was ready, he sent his servant to tell the guests, 'Come, the banquet is ready.' But they all began making excuses. One said, 'I have just bought a field and must inspect it. Please excuse me.' Another said, 'I have just bought five pairs of oxen, and I want to try them out. Please excuse me.' Another said, 'I now have a wife, so I can't come.' The servant returned and told his master what they had said. His master was furious and said, 'Go quickly into the streets and alleys of the town and invite the poor, the crippled, the blind, and the lame.' After the servant had done this, he reported, 'There is still room for more.' So his master said, 'Go out into the country lanes and behind the hedges and urge anyone you find to come, so that the house will be full. For none of those I first invited will get even the smallest taste of my banquet.'"

—LUKE 14:15–24 (NLT)

I WAS FIFTEEN YEARS old when the Martin Luther King Jr. holiday first became the law of the land. Having lived my entire childhood in Georgia, also Dr. King's birthplace, I knew his story and his heroics very well. I also knew that he was often maligned, sometimes viciously. So when that first official King Day rolled around on the calendar, it produced some very brisk conversations within my extended family, my community (a community that always had an element of the Ku Klux Klan lurking beneath its respectable surface), and yes, it produced some reaction within my childhood church.

Never can I forget standing outside the church sanctuary on a cold Sunday night, a nosey and curious teenager listening to the old men talk, just weeks before that first January observance of the King Holiday. One man asked the group, "Well, what y'all boys think about getting a day off for this King fella'?" With a big, fat, leather-bound King James Bible under his arm, and a plug of tobacco in his mouth, one of the other men answered, "Oh, I appreciate a day off. In fact, if we kill a few more of 'em, we might get a whole week off next year!" This was met by uproarious laughter and backslapping from the rest of the group. Then they all marched inside to sing praises to Jesus, apparently with clear consciences.

This attitude is very much alive in many circles, and that heinous joke is still laughed at in some Christian congregations; congregations that profess allegiance to Jesus, the same Jesus who welcomed all people regardless of their nationality, skin color, sexuality, gender, or any of the other factors that divide people. If we who are Christians are genuinely part of the church Jesus initiated, then love for our neighbor must be our calling card. Grace must be the currency which we exchange, and we who allege faith in Christ must be people of open arms and open doors to all people. Yes, this is the kingdom of God, alive and well on earth.

For me, this has become much more than theory or simple rhetoric. My adopted son is a multi-racial child. He and I together are, to quote Dr. King, "the sons of former slaves and the sons of former slave owners, from the red hills of Georgia."41 I want my son to grow up in a culture without the prejudice that has plagued these last hundreds of years. I want him to be a part of a nation where "he will not be judged by the color of his skin, but by the content of his character."42 But even if such achievements are not brought to bear in the greater society in his lifetime, for God's sake, I never want him subjected to the kind of conversation I heard as a teenager, all within the shadow of the church steeple. Regardless of what happens "out there," in the world, "in here," in the communion of faith, I want him—I want us all—to be a part of a community that welcomes those who are unlike ourselves. I want him to bear witness to radical acceptance, acceptance born of God's far-reaching grace.

Radical acceptance is the thesis that underlies this parable from Luke 14. As we continue to explore these dramatic stories of Jesus, we dive deeper into the living illustrations and characteristics that describe the reign of God. This story, the "Parable of the Banquet," is one of the deepest dives, and as I have explored elsewhere, it is likely Jesus' most profound story of all.43 It begins with a man throwing a party, and nobody shows up. To a person, every invited, distinguished guest begs off.

Well, socially this is completely unacceptable, so the host sends his servants out to the highways and byways to bring in all who will come: the vagrants, crack addicts, lepers, tax collectors, prostitutes, deviants, handicapped, and sick. These are all castaways, society's untouchables, and the barefaced oddballs who wander in off the street not knowing the difference between salad forks and hors d'oeuvres. They haven't a clue about table manners or cocktail party etiquette or how to behave at such an event as this. Yet, these people are made the guests of honor.

Meanwhile, those who had been invited previously—the ones who had good standing in the upper echelons of society, who had been born into the right families, who had the correct skin color, who were on the inside because of their wealth, their religion, their class, or their political connections—they find themselves outside on the street. Suddenly, the elite are the ones eating out of trash cans. They are the ones scrambling to find their next meal. They are the ones who try to fight off the cold of night with newspaper blankets and barrel fires. This reversal takes place not because the master of the feast, obviously God in Jesus' story, hates the fortunate members of society. It is because the fortunate refuse the invitation to come to the party that is the kingdom of God. But this good news is going to be celebrated with or without those initially invited. This party is for all who will enter the door, even those who do not know where the door is.

The explanation of this parable is obvious: while there is often no room in our religious structures, churches, denominational systems, or in our hearts for the outsiders, God goes out of his way to find these exact people and invites them in as family. He has plenty of room in his house and in his heart for all. This is a world-shattering, upside-down story about the far-reaching, outrageous, scandalous grace of God. God makes no distinction, he is no "respecter of persons," the old familiar text says (Acts 10:34). God doesn't draw lines of separation; he summons people to the party.

I feel we sometimes make a terrible mistake in regard to God's invitation, confusing the "holy" with the "sacred."44 There is a huge difference between the two, and I want to keep the two words as far apart as possible. Human beings create what is sacred, *sacrum* in Latin. Now, you might recognize that *sacrum* is also the name of the bones composing your pelvis. The ancient Romans called this part of the human body "sacred." Why? It is where the reproductive organs are, and, particularly in the female, it is from where life springs. It was recognized as something that had to be protected. It had to be kept safe and secure. That is an excellent picture, actually, of how we employ sacredness. Human beings create sacred rituals that draw lines, build barriers, and protect our turf. We have to keep everything that we perceive as a threat safely at a distance to guard our life and future.

Two quick examples. Not long ago I was preparing to speak at a church and had my always-handy coffee cup with me. Without any thought, I sat it down on the pulpit while I was reviewing my sermon notes. This church had more than a lectern or podium. It was truly the "sacred desk." A person came up to me and said, "I would appreciate it if you removed your cup. This furniture is sacred." I complied but then added, "Yes, it is 'sacred,' but do you know why? Because it has been designated so by a church committee, not by God. God's holiness is not offended by a Styrofoam cup." (I didn't mean to be snarky, but I don't think this person became a fan.)

And the second example. During one of my first pastorates the congregation moved from a shabby little storefront to a beautiful, magnificent sanctuary. It was an incredible upgrade with actual pews, a baptistery, a steeple, and plenty of other sacred things. In our old location we had been picking up poor children in the housing projects—whites, blacks, Latinos, and Asian-Indians—and bringing them to church. It was a very diverse group, but they had a common denominator: they were tornadoes. You could turn these kids loose in an empty room and they could find something to destroy.

When we moved to our new building we kept picking up these children, but I wondered how long it would last, because church people typically don't like outsiders messing up their stuff. Well, it lasted until the first week of Vacation Bible School. On the third night of the week-long event one of the church mothers came to retrieve me from my office in a huff. She was outraged. "Preacher," she said, "I need you to come look at something right now!" So I did as I was instructed. She took me to a hallway and pointed at the wall and asked, "What are we going to do about that?" About two and a half feet off the floor was a path of dirt plastered against the white wall. It continued down the entire length of the hallway stopping at one of the classroom doors. A group of these "dirty little bus kids" as she called them, had run their hands down the wall as they walked to class, that's all. I knew then that those kids' days were numbered in the new building.

I offer this definition: the sacred is the ritualistic behavior of individuals and groups that splinters space, community, and relationships. The sacred creates boundaries and barriers to protect us from what we feel is threatening, or to keep what is threatening on the outside.

The holy, however, is something completely different. Something holy is something that is "whole." The root word is "health." In other words, holiness is something that cannot be divided. It is something that is complete, unbroken, and intact. Accordingly, holiness is not something defined by lines of segregation or by different shades of acceptance. It is defined by receptivity and welcome.

The holy doesn't alienate, it invites.
The holy doesn't separate, it welcomes.
The holy doesn't divide, it embraces.
The holy doesn't close, it opens.

Whereas what is sacred is a small restricted space that must be sheltered and guarded, the old Norse word for "holy" means "a large living room," where people are made to feel very much at home.

By these definitions, Jesus was and is holy. God is holy. The church *should* be holy. But none of these are sacred (by the above description). I pray that God makes us holy: whole, healthy, welcoming people! But I also pray that he never allows us to become a sacred people, for when we lose our ability to be hospitable, inviting the outsider in, we have lost our unique witness in the world.

I remember the importance of this distinction every time I visit a restaurant just down the road from my house, an old watering hole called Nick's. Nick's is a legendary seafood joint frequented by tourists, locals, fisherman, national figures, and the occasional celebrity. Aesthetically, and I say this with great affection, Nick's is not much to look at. The building is constructed from whitewashed concrete blocks that are decades old. The parking lot is often flooded with rainwater, and chickens roam about in the yard. The ceiling is too low for my liking, and the view of the surrounding bayou is obscured by windows a touch too dark.

So if you were driving by, uninformed and uninitiated regarding this establishment, you might think Nick's to be some notorious hole-in-the-wall dive, and keep driving. That would be your incalculable loss. For three generations, the Nick family has been serving glorious local seafood, shucking the best Gulf Coast oysters, and slinging the coldest brew around. The restaurateurs that operate this roadside oasis keep the parking lot flooded all right—flooded with cars. People just can't stay away. This has a lot to do with the food, of course, but that's not the main draw. The Nicks know how to make you feel welcome. They make you feel at home. And what the atmosphere lacks visually, it more than makes up for with sincere friendship. Now, this doesn't mean I like everything on the menu, the low ceiling, or all of the Auburn University paraphernalia hanging on the walls. But I love being there, and judging by the time it takes to get a table, I'm not the only one.

The church could learn a few things from the Nick family. Their success is not the result of clever marketing, pumping thousands of dollars into publicity campaigns, arguing that their food is better than some competitor down the street, or declaring that theirs is the only true restaurant in town. No, this family has discovered the real meaning of holiness: genuinely welcome people into your living room, surround them with love, and call them your friends. Such is the kingdom of God.

To believe in a holy God is to believe in a God with open arms to all who will come, and this parable demonstrates it better than anywhere else in the Scriptures. God has no turf or furniture or newly painted walls to protect; no fears to guard against; no threats to his well-being, his reputation or his wholeness. This gives him the unique capacity to open his arms and his heart to all who will come to him. That capacity can be ours as well, if we will have it. The question is, "Will we?" Or put another way: are we willing to trade in our sacredness for God's holiness? Now, don't say, "Yes, Amen!" too soon. You see, when we begin to welcome to the party those whom God has already welcomed, when we deconstruct sacred barriers for the holiness of open doors, things can get a little messy.

Back to the parable. The master of the banquet achieves his final goal. His dining hall is filled to overflowing with revelers and party-goers. The grills are firing, the wine is flowing, no food is wasted, no drink is poured out, and the band doesn't have to play to an empty room. But this had to be one disorderly, ill-mannered, uncultured crowd. They aren't fashionably dressed and smelling of Chanel and Calvin Klein. These are shabby, uncombed, and unshaven street people who smell like body odor and cheap wine. They don't work as stock brokers or engineers. They panhandle and squeegee windshields. They didn't show up in Mercedes Benzes or BMWs. They came pushing old shopping carts and dragging tattered canvas bags.

Yet, none of this seems to have caused any discomfort for the man who threw the party, again, obviously God in Jesus' telling of the story. He just keeps sending his servants out to bring in more and more of the hooligans and untouchables—the more the merrier. But I wonder if it didn't cause a few of his employees, trusted caterers, and regular bartenders to swallow hard, look around at the salty crowd, then at each other, and conclude that the old man had finally gone off his rocker.

- Who gives a party with a guest list like this?

- Where did he find so many people with so many problems like these?

- Why did he erase the class lines and remove the social boundaries?

- How are we ever going to clean up when this party is over?

- What happens if this whole sordid affair gets out of control?

- Who is going to explain what is going on here to the neighbors?

It was all a bit embarrassing.

Yes, sometimes when you throw a party, nobody shows; but sometimes people actually show up, and they want to party—really party. For example, my oldest son recently planned an end-of-the-school-year bash. He worked on the guest list, planned out the minute details of his agenda, and advertised all over the place. Finally the party was consummated and all these teenage boys flooded our home. I don't know if you have ever hosted a dozen teenage boys overnight at your house, but you really should give it a try. Once.

The party began with hundreds of dollars' worth of pizza, coolers filled with sugary drinks, tunes pumping out of iPods connected to booming speakers, and with a gaggle of teenage girls present, enough awkward, adolescent sexual tension to suffocate the entire room. After the usual scary movie, and after all the girls were sent home with their parents, the young men retreated to the backyard for the night with their tents, sleeping bags, and a little camp fire. My wife had already retreated to the bedroom at this point; neither her nor the dog's nerves could take it any longer. And so while she and the dog slept and the teenage boys did what teenage boys do, I patrolled the grounds.

I fell asleep on the couch about 2:00 a.m. and awoke about forty-five minutes later in a panic. There was an eerie orange light flickering through the back windows of the house. I went to the back porch, looked down across the yard and the scene that met my eyes was like something out of *The Lord of the Flies*.45 All these boys were running around in the backyard, shirtless and bare, cold pizza hanging from their mouths, and soda cans scattered all over creation like land mines. They were whooping and crying like banshees, black streaks across their faces and bodies, and the harmless little campfire had been transformed into a roaring inferno. Flames were dancing fifteen feet in the air. Boys were scattered all over the woods, and the only reason I knew they were even out there was because of their constant screaming and the light of their flashlights bouncing among the trees. I knew that the police, fire department, juvenile justice, and the National Guard were all certainly on their way.

A few hours later, after the sun had come up, I was standing in front of the coffee pot, thinking about washing my face in it, when Cindy and the dog emerged from the bedroom, their tails wagging and looking all rested. I must have given her a hard look, I can't imagine why, and she had the nerve to ask me, "What's wrong with you?"

"What's wrong with me? Everything is wrong with me! I've had all the party I can stand and I can't stand anymore! So if you are going to remain in the kitchen with me, please be aware of my condition, and have a little compassion for what I have been through!" She went back to bed and I started making pancakes for the animals in the backyard, throwing them down from the back porch like they were Frisbees.

Through it all, do you know what my biggest concern was? Not the kids; they were being kids. Not my lack of sleep; I can catch up on that. It was the neighbors. "My God, what are they going to think of us?" was the constant worry on my mind.

It's no different within the church. Whenever we start moving away from the sacred and toward the holy we get uncomfortable with those we meet, of course, but we get even more uncomfortable with what other people who have shared our sacred standards will think about it all. When we welcome the outsider, those who have been our neighbors will react with misgiving. They might accuse us of all manner of unorthodoxy and heresy. They might even attempt to put us on the outside as well.46

Even so, these questions remain to be answered:

- Are we willing to bear this discomfort, and the scorn of others?

- Are we willing to become personally uncomfortable in order to welcome those to whom God has already opened his heart?

- Are we willing to bear the suspicion of our neighbors whom we have loved and known for so long?

- Are we willing to act and behave as Jesus?

Jesus never seemed to make decisions like he was filtering people out, putting some in the salvageable category and others in the discard pile. He never made decisions as if he were made uneasy or embarrassed by those who would answer his invitation. In fact, he went out of the way to welcome the weak and grab hold of those who were hanging on by less than a thread. Jesus was forever healing the sick, ministering to the poor, sticking up for the downtrodden, and crashing up against the shame and reward systems of his day. Why? Because Jesus recognized that some people just don't have a chance unless the door is opened to them and they are invited in. They are too feeble to pull themselves up by their own bootstraps or too poor to hire the best attorneys. They are too small to stick it to the system or too unconnected to call in any favors. They don't know enough, aren't strong enough, and can't recover fast enough. They are untouchable, forgotten, stigmatized, diseased, ostracized, rejected, and helpless.

But they are welcomed with open arms. That is world-changing, status quo-shattering holiness. God help us to say and be the same.

Chapter 8

For the Long Haul

"The Kingdom of Heaven will be like ten bridesmaids who took their lamps and went to meet the bridegroom. Five of them were foolish, and five were wise. The five who were foolish didn't take enough olive oil for their lamps, but the other five were wise enough to take along extra oil. When the bridegroom was delayed, they all became drowsy and fell asleep. At midnight they were roused by the shout, 'Look, the bridegroom is coming! Come out and meet him!' All the bridesmaids got up and prepared their lamps. Then the five foolish ones asked the others, 'Please give us some of your oil because our lamps are going out.' But the others replied, 'We don't have enough for all of us. Go to a shop and buy some for yourselves.' But while they were gone to buy oil, the bridegroom came. Then those who were ready went in with him to the marriage feast, and the door was locked. Later, when the other five bridesmaids returned, they stood outside, calling, 'Lord! Lord! Open the door for us!' But he called back, 'Believe me, I don't know you!' So you, too, must keep watch! For you do not know the day or hour of my return."

—MATTHEW 25:1–13 (NLT)

ON OCTOBER 30, 1938, millions of ordinary Americans were convinced that the world was coming to an end. This was not because of events transpiring in Europe, as Hitler rattled his sabers and the entire world teetered on the verge of war. Rather, these fears were fueled by a fictional broadcast aired from a small CBS radio studio in New York City. Orson Welles was on the air that night as the usual host of the Mercury Theater. He was using the science fiction book *War of the Worlds* as his script.47 Welles described in dramatic and fictional detail—with that unmistakable voice of his—how Martians had invaded Earth, landing in Grover's Mill, New Jersey.

An excerpt from Orson Welles' reading that night goes like this: "Ladies and gentlemen, I have a grave announcement to make. Incredible as it may seem, both the observations of science and the evidence of our eyes leads to the inescapable assumption that those strange beings who landed in the New Jersey farmlands tonight are the vanguard of an invading army from the planet Mars. The battle which took place tonight at Grover's Mill has ended in one of the most startling defeats suffered by an army in modern times. Seven thousand men armed with rifles and machine-guns pitted against a single fighting machine of the invaders from Mars. There are only one hundred and twenty known survivors."48

There were thirty-two million listeners that evening, and none with twenty-four hour news, Twitter, Google, or text messages to learn from the world around them. As a result, the nation was thrown into a terrifying panic. Telephone lines were clogged, police stations were overrun, the military was put on alert, anxious mobs filled the streets, churches ran over with impromptu prayer meetings, citizens barricaded and armed themselves.

Research journals, doctoral dissertations, and multiple volumes of books have been written on the fear, paranoia, and social upheaval unveiled by Welles and his cast on that single October night. It was a type of unnerving hysteria that simply could not be duplicated today.

There is a Christian equivalent to this kind of panic, spewed from radio and television stations, podcasts, pulpits, books, periodicals, and websites. This oft-presented Christian version of the Apocalypse is initiated not by a Martian invasion, but by Jesus' violent and destructive return to earth. "Jesus is coming back," the evangelists say, "he is mad as hell, and he plans to send you there! There won't be many survivors, but if you do survive, you will be left behind to suffer the rage and vengeance of the glory of the Lord, as he 'tramples out the vintage where the grapes of wrath are stored.'"

Some of the Orson Welleses of our day are leading evangelicals like Tim LaHaye and Jerry Jenkins, writers of the *Left Behind* series.49 LaHaye and Jenkins have completed a collection of sixteen books, now among the best-selling books of Christian fiction ever written. More than sixty-five million copies have been sold, and they have movies, computer games, CDs, audios, videos, kids' books, T-shirts, calendars, and greeting cards. They have prophetic fear shrink-wrapped, pre-packaged, and ready for shipment. Their doomsdaying has created a kind of neurotic anxiety within some circles of Christianity, as faithful readers can barely distinguish the truth of today's headlines from the fiction (and it is *fiction*) of a New York Times Best Seller.50

Personally, I'm very well acquainted with this kind of hysteria (to which I have already referred). Growing up in a fundamental and revivalistic tradition, every few weeks the pastor would serve up a good dose of Cyrus Scofield or Hal Lindsey mixed in with John the Revelator and Ezekiel's Battle of Gog and Magog; telling us how the universe was about to come unwrapped and how very few of us were going to make it in. I can't tell you how many times I heard a preacher say something like, "The Lord Jesus could return at any moment! He could return before I finish preaching this morning!" And then the speaker would preach for so long, I thought that's exactly what he was trying to achieve: preach till Jesus got there.

I didn't like this sort of exhortation. I was, after all, a teenager being told how big a sinner I was, but I didn't feel like I had gotten to sin very much yet. I hadn't got to do much of anything! I hadn't traveled, hadn't earned my driver's license, hadn't fallen in love, hadn't acquired legal age, or really even lived. If Jesus had been content to wait all these centuries to return to earth, just to show up at this particular blip in history to interrupt my simple little plans, then I concluded it would be a raw deal.

My feelings about so much of the "Second Coming" preaching I hear still makes me cranky (but for a different reason than when I was a teenager). We are so absolutely convinced that we are living in the final chapter of human history—on the last page, if not within the last paragraph—that we are in danger of giving away the future.

This said, I turn to a parable that revivalists have absolutely worn out over the years, prepping the world for the impending arrival of Christ. It is a parable traditionally known as the "Parable of the Ten Virgins," though these young ladies' chastity is hardly an issue in the story. The New Living Translation is more accurate: these young ladies are bridesmaids waiting for a wedding to begin. Yes, some have made it an apocalyptic centerpiece—and Jesus does say that this is what the kingdom of God will be like in the future—but I think that the future has already arrived. If we look at this parable from a different perspective, we will see that we are already there. So let's take a closer look at this story, a look that puts us in the future about which Jesus was speaking.

First, this is an ancient Jewish story that is not embedded in our modern Western culture. That's one of the reasons this parable strikes us as so strange; but it's not strange really, for this type of wedding scenario was common in Jesus' day. Jewish marriages of the period were fulfilled in three distinct stages: engagement, betrothal, and the actual marriage. The engagement could be an extended period lasting years. Marriages were often pre-arranged by the parents, so engagements could begin while the prospective couple were still children. This engagement period was followed by an official betrothal period. The betrothal lasted for a year, and while the couple did not yet live together, the two were considered bound together in marriage. Following the engagement and betrothal, having spanned many years, the actual marriage ceremony finally took place. But even then, the ceremony was nothing like what we observe in our culture. The nuptials took a long, long time.

In that culture it was impossible to RSVP at a specific time for the ceremony, as there was no specific time given. As the wedding day drew near, an announcement would be made to the entire village: "The groom is on his way for his bride!" This would put all the gears in motion: cooking, cleaning, reserving the banquet hall, donning the wedding garments, and putting everyone on alert, including the bride and her bridesmaids as in this story. But the announcement, "the groom is on his way," was very general. He might be a mile away, several days' journey away, finishing with sowing his wild oats at an extended bachelor party, or more than likely, in protracted negotiations with the bride's father.

It was not unusual for the father of the bride and the groom to be haggling over the "price" of the bride and her dowry. This was a delicate matter. If the groom offered too little, then he offended her father. If the father gave in too quickly, it communicated that he didn't prize his daughter or that he wanted her out of the house as quickly as possible. It sounds callous, but this was a business negotiation as much as anything else, and a great deal of arbitration was involved. Arbitration, thusly, took time.

All of this is playing out in the background of Jesus' story, and his original listeners would have understood this instinctively. Similar customs, while unfamiliar to those of us living in North America, are still followed in tribal and Eastern traditions today. It was as common for them as bridal showers, white gowns, and tuxedoes are common for us.

So, it is in this context that Jesus' story is told. The groom is on his way and the entire village has been put on alert. This includes the bridesmaids, whose job it is to accompany the bride to her wedding ceremony. These young ladies would walk with her to the celebration and accompany her every step of the way. Sometimes, as in Jesus' story, the groom arrived at the most inconvenient hour, even in the middle of the night. If that was the case, then the bridesmaids would ignite their lamps, join the bridal procession and provide light for the path. This was both practical and ceremonial. People needed to see where to step, yes, but an official and ready lamp in a young woman's hand communicated that she was indeed a bridesmaid and that she belonged there. She was known by the bride and was a welcome friend. This is where the ten young ladies with their lamps enter Jesus' story. They have a definite task: join the procession and light the way. That's why they are hanging out in the street carrying their lanterns and bottles of oil.

And it is here that I must depart from the usual apocalyptic interpretation of the parable. The point of this story is not that Jesus will come and rescue some while others are left behind. The point of this story is not that some were awake and others were asleep—they were all asleep. The point of this story is about the delay, the extremely long time it takes for the groom to finally arrive. The only difference between those who got to the wedding on time and those who did not is this: those who made it—those who were wise—anticipated a long delay on the part of the groom. They had extra oil for their lamps. The others—those who were foolish—had oil, but not an extra supply. They didn't have enough. They never believed it would take so long, thus they simply ran out of gas.

This parable only makes sense, especially with thousands of years of Christian history behind us, if we understand that this isn't a story about the imminent return of Christ. It is a story about his *delayed* return. In telling this story Jesus seems to be saying, "This world may not wrap up as quickly or as neatly as you think. The wait may be exceptionally long. You may not be standing at the end of human history at all. You might only be in the first few chapters or at the halfway mark. Be prepared for the long haul, for this isn't a sprint to the finish. It's not even a mid-distance run. This is a marathon, an ultramarathon, and you can't burn up all your fuel thinking the finish line is just over the horizon."

The wisdom of these five young ladies with the extra oil becomes clear, as they were not misled or unprepared for a lengthy wait. They were ready, and when the time came for them to light the darkness—the job they had been given all along—they had the fuel and resources to do so. They had not given up on their task; they were prepared for the long haul.

Unfortunately, the church has not always followed the wisdom of these young ladies in this parable. There have been startling, bizarre examples in Christian history of those who were so oblivious to the future, and so convinced of Jesus' imminent return, that they gave up on this life and this world completely, with disastrous consequences. One such man was a Baptist minister named William Miller. He was a preacher of some skill and a product of the Second Great Awakening that swept the frontier regions of the United States in the 1800s. With apocalyptic and religious enthusiasm in the air, like many Christians of the time period, Miller became fixated on the second coming of Christ. He began studying the prophetic books of the Bible, particularly the books of Daniel and

Revelation, and through a very complex set of calculations, Miller concluded that "the second coming of Jesus Christ is near, even at the door . . . on or before 1844."51

A few of Miller's associates were bold enough to stamp the world with a more exact expiration date: October 22, 1844. Magazines were printed, camp meetings were held, and fifteen hundred Millerite evangelists scoured the countryside with the word that the end was near. Miller's ideas gained incredible traction. A million people—an extraordinary number for the time—attended his meetings, and thousands were converted to his ideas. Then, on the evening of October 21, 1844, as many as a hundred thousand of William Miller's followers gathered on hillsides all over the country to mark the big event they called the "Midnight Cry." The bridegroom was coming in the night, just like this parable. They had quit their jobs, had given away all their possessions, had made peace with God, and many were wearing white robes, ready to welcome Jesus back to earth.

Nothing happened, of course, and in Millerite history October 22, 1844, became known as "The Great Disappointment," rather than the Great Day of the Lord. The Millerites had become, in the words of the cliché, "so heavenly minded, they were of no earthly good."

I wish I could say that Miller was an isolated case, but we know differently. And it's not just a few flakey groups on the periphery, men like Harold Camping or Pat Robertson or some other yo-yo. It's "normal" people who look around at this crazy world (and I can hardly blame them), and they want the Ferris wheel to stop so that they can get off. They are like the preachers of my childhood who were good-hearted and so very well intentioned, but they couldn't face the world as it really was. They are like friends of mine from college who became so convinced Jesus would return before they were thirty—the year 2000—that they dropped out of school and began preparing for the big checkout. They are like the man whose middle-school children were in my church youth group when I was a youth minister. He quit saving for their education because he "knew that Jesus would return before they got out of high school." Those children now have children of their own.

On and on it goes, our view of the future grows darker and more sinister, our hope fades away, and the timeline we attach to the world is never beyond a few fleeting days. Are we not playing the role of the foolish bridesmaids who are simply unprepared for the long haul? Rather than asking the evangelist's question, "What if Jesus came back today?" we would be better served by asking, "What if he doesn't?"

What if Jesus does not come back today . . .
or tomorrow . . .
or next year . . .
or next decade . . .
or next century?

What kind of world do we want our descendants to be living in? What kind of world will we have then? If we aren't prepared to light the way into a distant future—for the long haul—then we aren't very wise, and we certainly aren't very faithful to our calling as citizens of the kingdom of God. We become little more than caricatures of today's politicians who choose to kick society's worst problems down the street for another generation to address, long after they have left office. We become freakish doomsday-preppers who misunderstand that the best preparation is to join God in his transforming work rather than watching the clock for the end of the world.

Maybe we could take a lesson from a different clock being built by a not-for-profit organization called "The Long Now Foundation." This organization has been around since 1996, and it hopes to be around much, much longer. The Long Now Foundation has one essential goal: to reverse the trend in our culture of short-term thinking.

The founders, who are from all over the professional spectrum, believe that our "accelerating technology, the short-horizon perspective of market-driven economics, the next-election perspective of democracies, and the distractions of personal multi-tasking" have given us "a pathologically short attention span." They want to provide some sort of corrective balance to our short-sightedness and encourage "the long view and the taking of long-term responsibility, where 'long-term' is measured in centuries, not months, years, or even decades."52

Daniel Hillis, one of the founders of Long Now says, "When I was a child, people used to talk about what would happen by the year 2000 . . . and now no one mentions a future date at all. I think it is time for us to start a long-term project that gets people thinking past the mental barrier of an ever-shortening future."53 That long-term project is the building of a massive clock that will tick for the next ten thousand years. The clock is currently under construction and will be placed in a cave in the Great Basin National Park in Nevada. It is hundreds of feet tall, a beautifully elaborate twenty-first century version of Stonehenge, with chimes designed to play a different tune every time it strikes. Human civilization is about ten thousand years old now, so a ten-thousand-year-old clock says, quite optimistically, that we are only getting started. The point of the clock is not to mark time, but to rekindle our hope in and enthusiasm for the future.

The church, allegedly the most hopeful community in the world, could use some of that thinking. Granted, such thinking goes against everything many of us have been taught, especially if our particular tradition is swamped with apocalyptic terror, but unlearning some of what we have been taught is now necessary. The truth is that Jesus will probably not return today, and it's not likely he will return in our lifetimes. Therefore, we have to be more than prepared for his coming. We must be prepared to persevere. No, "God is not slow about keeping his promises," but do not miss what I believe to be Jesus' point with this story: no matter how long the darkness lasts and no matter how long the wait, the kingdom task of the follower of Christ remains the same. We have to persist in our assigned task of illuminating the darkness, knowing that the wait will likely be longer than many sincere people could ever imagine.

The work of this ongoing task may indeed be required of us for a long, long time. Let us be found always faithful in giving light to a world that needs it.

Chapter 9

(Un)Doing Justice

"The kingdom is also like what happened when a man went away and put his three servants in charge of all he owned. The man knew what each servant could do. So he handed five thousand coins to the first servant, two thousand to the second, and one thousand to the third. Then he left the country. As soon as the man had gone, the servant with the five thousand coins used them to earn five thousand more. The servant who had two thousand coins did the same with his money and earned two thousand more. But the servant with one thousand coins dug a hole and hid his master's money in the ground. Some time later the master of those servants returned. He called them in and asked what they had done with his money. The servant who had been given five thousand coins brought them in with the five thousand that he had earned. He said, 'Sir, you gave me five thousand coins, and I have earned five thousand more.' 'Wonderful!' his master replied. 'You are a good and faithful servant. I left you in charge of only a little, but now I will put you in charge of much more. Come and share in my happiness!' Next, the servant who had been given two thousand coins came in and said, 'Sir, you gave me two thousand coins, and I have earned two thousand more.' 'Wonderful!' his master replied. 'You are a good and faithful servant. I left you in charge of only a little, but now I will put you in charge of much more. Come and share in my happiness!' The servant who had been given one thousand coins then came in and said, 'Sir, I know that you are hard to get along with.

You harvest what you don't plant and gather crops where you haven't scattered seed. I was frightened and went out and hid your money in the ground. Here is every single coin!' The master of the servant told him, 'You are lazy and good-for-nothing! You know that I harvest what I don't plant and gather crops where I haven't scattered seed. You could have at least put my money in the bank, so that I could have earned interest on it.' Then the master said, 'Now your money will be taken away and given to the servant with ten thousand coins! Everyone who has something will be given more, and they will have more than enough. But everything will be taken from those who don't have anything. You are a worthless servant, and you will be thrown out into the dark where people will cry and grit their teeth in pain.'"

—MATTHEW 25:14–30 (CEV)

NOT LONG AGO I had the opportunity to hear that young, bespectacled, dreadlocked radical author and speaker Shane Claiborne give a talk. If you are not acquainted with Shane, you should be. He is a remarkable young man who leads the Christian community known as "The Simple Way" in Philadelphia, Pennsylvania; and beyond his pastoral and prophetic roles, he works on behalf of his city's poor. His activism has gotten him into trouble through the years, even landing him in jail a number of times. He is courageous enough to participate in civil disobedience, or what he calls "holy trespassing," to speak against the powers that be. He is a thoughtful man, a true revolutionary, and an instigator of justice. He is also a great storyteller.

One of the stories I heard him tell came right from the city he calls home. By Shane's testimony, the city of Philadelphia is very severe when it comes to homeless issues. If you hand out food on the street without a restaurant permit, for example, you risk being fined or going to jail. Further, if you invite the homeless in off the street, and your facility has not been approved as an official shelter, the city will shut you down or take you to court. They have made it very difficult to help people. Shane shared what one group of committed Christians decided to do about this problem. It was a little group of Pentecostals trying to shelter people from the elements. The city came in and said, "You can't do that. You don't have a permit. Your facility isn't designed for this." So, as good Pentecostals are prone to do, they prayed about it for a week.

At the end of that week they held a public news conference and announced that they would in fact shut down their shelter to comply with the city ordinance. But they didn't want their facility to go unused, so they announced that they were opening a church instead; a church that would hold services nightly. Then they invited everyone to the church service that very evening. After a couple of hours of preaching, testimonies, gospel singing, and communion, the leader stood and announced, "This concludes the formal portion of our service. The next eight hours will be set aside for silent meditation and reflection." He implored the group that if they should notice someone with their eyes closed, lying down on a pew or a cot, to leave them alone—they were communing with God! With a bit of divine imagination, this group found a way to subvert the ways of the world and redeem an unjust situation, even if in time they might have to pay a steep price for it.54

There comes a time, when confronted by the realities around us, that the best confession we can make is this: "We will not play by the rules that an unjust society has constructed. We will not be partners with, be party to, or perpetuate injustice and wrongdoing. We will find a different way—a redemptive way—to live in the world. We will be the people of God's kingdom, which means we will throw light on what is unjust and dark, and then creatively do something about it, even if suffering the consequences for those actions might be required."

This parable, "The Parable of the Talents," as it is sometimes known, is a kingdom story about just such a confession, even though this familiar story is traditionally not read in this sort of light.

A wealthy nobleman leaves three of his servants in charge of his business affairs. Each servant receives a denomination of money. Two of the three invest the money and experience incredible success. The third does nothing with the money and experiences an equally incredible penalty for his failure. The customary application is clear: you'd better do something with the talent, time, and resources that God has given you, because one day Jesus will return and you will have to give an answer for yourself. But I propose that this interpretation is inaccurate, and the third servant has been mistakenly vilified.

The prevailing interpretation of this parable is the result of the presuppositions we bring to the story. We have always read this story—and we can't help it, it's who we are—as Americans. It is ingrained in us, socially and economically, to make a profit.

> Be responsible.
> Be productive.
> Increase the bottom line.
> Meet next quarter's sales projections.
> Successful people make money, and a lot of it.

An audience with such presuppositions was not present when Jesus first spoke these words, and while this may surprise some readers, Jesus wasn't a capitalist, and his first hearers were not Americans. They had never read Adam Smith or John Locke, or had a course in Western democracy; and the entrepreneurial idea of contemporary *laissez faire* economics was quite foreign to them. We hear this story from a position of empowerment and conclude that God sanctions our culture of competition and achievement. The first audience heard this story from a position of weakness and vulnerability, a culture of survival. This change of perspective, putting ourselves into the first hearers' position, changes everything.

Wealthy landowners were not viewed by the general populace as the great heroes of enterprise. They were viewed with suspicion, often disgust and hate, because at the time of Jesus there were only two classes—the "haves," a very small percentage of the population protected by their money, gated walls, and their exploitation of the weak, and the "have-nots," the vast majority of the population who were struggling to stay alive. The "have-nots" lived on a subsistence basis, concluding that if someone has too much stuff, then someone else in the community did not have enough.

So this makes the wealthy landowner in this story not a picture of a benevolent God who has entrusted resources to his servants who then scurry off to earn the virtuous words, "Well done, my good and faithful servant." No, this makes this man a greedy, villainous aristocrat. He is a man who has "reaped where he did not sow and gathered where he scattered no seed" (verse 26). Reflecting a common practice in the first century, he was likely a land baron who loaned money to the poor peasant farmers at grotesque levels of interest, and when they could not pay their bills, he kicked them off their land or repossessed his losses in the form of their crops while they got nothing for their hard work. We can imagine him to be a gangster, a crook, a racketeer, a loan-sharking extortionist who perpetuated a vile system of sharecropping and indentured slavery, breaking the society—he reaped what he did not sow.55

It's not unrealistic to imagine this man gaining his wealth through terrifying means. Injustice toward the local farmers, repossession of their land, extreme rates of interest, cruelty to their families: this was everything that the law prohibited. The Jewish economic system, and this will offend us capitalists even further, was designed to prevent these types of inequities. Exorbitant interest was not allowed (there were no twenty-one percent credit cards or payday title pawns). Benevolence toward the poor, the widows, and the orphans was commanded. Every seven years, according to Mosaic Law, all debts were cancelled and everybody got a clean financial slate. And every fifty years, at the end of seven seven-year cycles, Jewish society celebrated the Year of Jubilee. All debts were forgiven, all slaves were set free, all indentured servants were returned to their families, and all land was returned to its original owners. It was an economic and social reboot that wiped away all inequality. It sounds like madness to us who live in an extremely individualistic "what's-mine-is-mine, pull-yourself-up-by-your-bootstraps" culture, but this is the economics God intended for the Jewish people.

Therefore, for some to gain excessive wealth in this system, they *had* to be violating the law and taking advantage of people (the landowner betrays this fact with his own words), and this man had gained obscene wealth. In the original text, he hands over a total of eight talents to his servants. A talent was not ability, it was money. One talent was the equivalent of fifteen to twenty years' salary. This is upwards of eight to ten million dollars by today's standards, and in the short time that the master of the house is away, the two "faithful servants" double this sum. The only way they could have done that was to perpetuate the unjust practices that had acquired so much wealth in the first place.56

So by returning to the cultural setting of the first century and Jesus' first hearers, we are prevented from running as quickly as possible to make this a parable about a God who prefers and rewards free enterprise economics over all other systems. Rather, this is a parable about how we who are residents of the kingdom of God face the systematic injustices that surround us. How do we react when we find ourselves connected to people and organizations that participate in injustice, inequality, and wrong-doing?

Here is an answer, from the text itself, if we can hear the story retold, exchanging our cultural lenses for the lenses worn by those in Jesus' day. This does more than just update the cultural context over twenty centuries. It actually changes the entire meaning, application, and implications of the parable. So, consider the story told like this:

The President and General Partner of a successful hedge fund had to travel overseas to conduct business in the emerging Asian markets. He called three of his fund managers together, and gave each one responsibility for the growth of his investors' money during his absence. One manager received ten billion dollars to manage; the next received five billion; and the last received one billion. Quickly, the first two managers put their money to work. Leveraging derivatives, options, and futures; taking advantage of trends in the housing market and demands for petroleum products; capitalizing on rising food prices and threats of unrest; and using complex trading algorithms while thumbing their noses at ethics, these two managers each doubled their money in no time at all. Meanwhile, the third manager rented a safe deposit box, stuffed his money and treasury notes inside and did nothing.

When the President returned, he called his fund managers to account. The first manager reported that his portfolio was now worth twenty billion dollars. The President was ecstatic! "Well done," he said. "Please, make plans to join me in the Hamptons next weekend, and together we will celebrate our great success and officially promote you to partner in the firm. You have earned it, my friend."

Of course, the second manager was just as successful. He too had doubled the size of the investments entrusted to him. "Well done, my good man," the President crowed. "We will soon enjoy an island vacation on my private yacht. Bring your family. They will want to enjoy the fruits of your labors as well. You have a very bright future with this firm."

Then the third manager was called to the penthouse office of the President. He stood before the great oaken desk, his knees knocking just above the Persian rug beneath his feet, and thrusting a briefcase forward, he said, "Sir, here is your money, every penny you entrusted to me, and not a penny less. I fear that you are a hard, calloused man who makes money by taking advantage of people. You have grown rich off the hard work of people beneath you and by manipulating the system in your favor. I refuse to participate in your unethical and unjust efforts at making money at the expense of others."

The President was outraged, not only because a portion of his hedge fund would show no gains for the previous quarter, a fact that would not be missed by his investors, but also because one of his employees would dare speak to him in such a fashion.

"You ungrateful, unmotivated, bleeding heart! Who do you think you are? You know how things work around here! Clean out your office. Turn in your keys to the company car, the company credit accounts, and all company technologies. Be out of the corporate apartment by lunchtime today. Consider these words your severance pay. I'll make sure you never work in this town again. Now get out of my sight. You can starve in the streets for all I care."

And as the now-unemployed fund manager is escorted from the room by well-armed security, his vacated portfolio is handed over to the new junior partner, who would actually make some money with it.

Does my retelling of the story push the parable too far? I don't think so. The landowner could very well be an unethical Wall Street trader; a wealthy cotton farmer perpetuating black slavery or Jim Crow; a mobster shaking down the shop owners on his street; a sharkish CEO who holds his employees hostage with crooked bonuses and cooked books; a politician who uses coercive power to get what he wants; a pastor or religious leader who manipulates the masses and demands total allegiance from his lieutenants; or a school administrator who plays favorites for his own benefit and requires those who wish to be his favorites to play the game. The villain in this story is anyone who uses his or her position to take advantage of others, whether by means of money, power, sex, race, gender, religion, class, politics, or a thousand other shame-and-reward tools of intimidation.

In light of this, do we then understand the implication of this parable?

What did the third manager in the story, the one usually regarded as the poor example but who we must now view as the tragic hero of the tale, do? He refused to participate in or cooperate with what would hurt others, no matter how much he stood to gain personally, and no matter how much he stood to lose by refusing to do so! He simply refused to join forces with injustice. He understood that sometimes the greatest act of justice is achieved by inaction.

Summarizing John Howard Yoder on this subject, when a system of power becomes incorrigible, the disciple of Jesus Christ most effectively takes responsibility by refusing to collaborate with such a system. This refusal takes the side "of the victims whom power is oppressing."57

If we see that the world is a greedy, dog-eat-dog place, we can't just complain about it. We might have to quit working for, propping up, and giving our silent consent to people and organizations that glorify and advance greed. If we see injustice thriving in our workplace, in our community, or in our church, when people are being mistreated, maligned, or taken advantage of, we have to stop being "yes" men and women, and say, "No. I refuse to help you hurt others."

Sometimes we have to admit that because we follow Christ and are citizens in the kingdom of God, the rationale "that's just the way it is," is not near enough motivation or excuse to keep going with the flow. When we see that the actions and practices of a person, company, employer, institution, or group brings harm to others, we should quit collaborating with those who reap what they did not sow. Whenever we stand to gain by someone else being treated unjustly, then we have violated the most basic tenant of our faith: we are not treating others as we want to be treated, and we are not loving our neighbors as we love ourselves. When we just let things go where they will, we can become active participants in wrongdoing, and that's not right.

After all, how can we expect the world to be any different if we don't believe and act differently ourselves? How can we expect the world to change if we don't change? How can we expect to stem the tide of injustice if we aren't willing to go against the flow every now and then? There simply comes a time when the greatest action we can take is the refusal to act or participate any longer.

My suspicion is that we do not need to draw out the implications of this parable too forcefully, for we see very clearly what will happen if we begin to stand against those who abuse their power. We might get blackballed, fired, kicked to the curb, or lose our financial security. We might have to creatively defy a city's unjust ordinance or consider our own acts of "holy trespassing." Frankly, it just might cost us something to live like this. But where did we think carrying the cross of Jesus would lead us in the first place? Those who carry a cross are obviously headed toward some kind of crucifixion. But crucifixions are required for love to be resurrected in the world, and when love is set loose by just a few, it bears the fruit of change, justice, and restoration for all.

I'll conclude these thoughts and this chapter with what might be considered a dramatic account: the account of Father Oscar Romero. Romero entered the priesthood as a young man, and for many decades he served quietly and uneventfully, managing the status quo of his church and his world. This "make no waves" attitude eventually led to his appointment as archbishop of his home country of El Salvador in 1977. This was a time of great upheaval in the country. The right-wing militaristic government and the left-wing rebels had begun a civil war that would eventually inflame the entire region and cost the lives of seventy-five thousand people. It was felt that Romero would go about his work as he always had and stay out of the way.

At first, Romero did exactly that. But then his dear friend, Father Rutilio Grande was assassinated by the government for speaking out against the violence being waged against the poor and innocent of the country, particularly the children. This assassination changed Romero profoundly, and as leader of the Catholic Church in the region, he realized he could no longer go along with the way things were. He began to speak out. He began to pull himself away from the oppressive systems that asked him to give his silent assent. He could no longer be a participant in injustice.

In a February 1980 speech he said, "In less than three years, more than fifty priests have been attacked and threatened. . . . Six are already martyred; they were murdered. Some have been tortured and others expelled. Nuns have also been persecuted. The archdiocesan radio station and educational institutions that are of a Christian inspiration have been attacked, threatened, intimidated, even bombed. Several parish communities have been raided. . . . But it is important to note why [the Church] has been persecuted. Not any and every priest has been persecuted, not any and every institution has been attacked. That part of the church has been attacked and persecuted that put itself on the side of the people, [specifically], the poor."58

A month later Father Romero delivered his last sermon, broadcast by radio across El Salvador. He appealed for Christians to behave as Christians, for believers to reflect the kingdom of God, and for Jesus' followers to refuse "being used to further worldly ambitions." And then he spoke the words that sealed his fate: "I would like to make a special appeal to the men of the army, and specifically to the ranks of the National Guard, the police, and the military. Brothers, you are killing your own brothers. . . . No soldier is obliged to obey an order contrary to the law of God. No one has to obey an immoral law. It is high time you recovered your consciences and obeyed your consciences rather than a sinful order. The church, the defender of the rights of God, of the law of God, of human dignity, of the person, cannot remain silent before such an abomination. . . . In the name of God, in the name of this suffering people whose cries rise to heaven more loudly each day, I implore you, I beg you, I order you in the name of God: stop the repression."59

That very night the assassination plot against Romero was devised at the highest levels of the Salvadoran government. The next day, as Father Romero served the Holy Eucharist at a hospital chapel, he was gunned down. The bread and the chalice were still held in his hand. No one was ever charged or prosecuted, and it took thirty years for the Salvadoran government to issue an apology and confession of the wrongdoing.

Did Romero know the personal dangers he faced in refusing to go along? Absolutely. Just weeks before his murder he said, "I am bound by divine command to give my life for those whom I love, and that includes all Salvadorans, even those who are going to kill me. . . . If they kill me, I shall rise in the Salvadoran people. I offer my blood for the redemption and resurrection of El Salvador."60

Is this a dramatic conclusion? Yes, but this is a dramatic parable that calls us to dramatic life-giving sacrifice as we learn what it means to trespass with holiness and to "do what is right, love being kind to others, and live humbly, obeying our God" (Micah 6:6 CEV).

Chapter 10

"Go to Jesus!"

"When he finally arrives, blazing in beauty and all his angels with him, the Son of Man will take his place on his glorious throne. Then all the nations will be arranged before him and he will sort the people out, much as a shepherd sorts out sheep and goats, putting sheep to his right and goats to his left. Then the King will say to those on his right, 'Enter, you who are blessed by my Father! Take what's coming to you in this kingdom. It's been ready for you since the world's foundation. And here's why: I was hungry and you fed me, I was thirsty and you gave me a drink, I was homeless and you gave me a room, I was shivering and you gave me clothes, I was sick and you stopped to visit, I was in prison and you came to me.' Then those 'sheep' are going to say, 'Master, what are you talking about? When did we ever see you hungry and feed you, thirsty and give you a drink? And when did we ever see you sick or in prison and come to you?' Then the King will say, 'I'm telling the solemn truth: Whenever you did one of these things to someone overlooked or ignored, that was me—you did it to me.' Then he will turn to the 'goats,' the ones on his left, and say, 'Get out, worthless goats! You're good for nothing but the fires of hell. And why? Because—I was hungry and you gave me no meal, I was thirsty and you gave me no drink, I was homeless and you gave me no bed, I was shivering and you gave me no clothes, Sick and in prison, and you never visited.' Then those 'goats' are going to say, 'Master, what are you talking about? When did we ever see you hungry or thirsty or homeless or shivering or sick or in prison and didn't help?' He will answer them, 'I'm telling the solemn truth: Whenever you failed to do one of these things to someone who was being overlooked or ignored, that was me—you failed to do it to me.' Then those 'goats' will be herded to their eternal doom, but the 'sheep' to their eternal reward."

—MATTHEW 25:31–46 (THE MESSAGE)

I WAS ONCE SMACKED away from the dinner table. Now don't make a call to child protective services, because I was never abused, not even close. But my parents did believe in the effectiveness of that proverb, "Spare the rod, spoil the child." So I was definitely not spoiled. And even if corporal punishment had not been practiced in my childhood home, I still would not have been over-indulged. My father often worked two jobs in the textile mills to pay the bills, and my mother cared for my youngest sibling who was very ill. There was always more month than money, and my poor wardrobe of patched blue jeans and worn-out tennis shoes proved as much—and sometimes, so did our diet.

On what felt like the umpteenth night in a row that my mother served us the culinary delights of macaroni and cheese and fish sticks, I just could not eat another serving of the Gorton's Fisher-man. So, not knowing the economic pressures of feeding a family on a meager income, I voiced my complaint: "Fish sticks, again! Is that all we have?" You can guess her response. She said, "Why don't you learn to be thankful! There are children all over the world who would love to have a fish stick to eat." You can also guess my unwise answer: "Well," I said, "Why don't you send those children my fish sticks, because I can't stand to eat another one." I discovered that a fish stick tastes pretty good with a fat lip. I also discovered the power of prayer.

I started secretly praying, that very night, for God to bring something to our table besides fish sticks or Hamburger Helper with only the "Helper." My prayers continued for some days, and then they were answered by one of my father's coworkers. His name was Bobby Gentry. Bobby was always lending a hand where he could: a small wad of cash stuffed into my dad's hand (usually with the instructions, "Here, take this for your family; you need it worse than the church does"); underwriting medical assistance for my ailing brother; or a weekend job for my dad. So just a few days after the fish stick episode, it was Bobby who pulled into the driveway of our home on a warm Saturday morning.

When he emerged from his car he was dressed as I had never seen him before. Rather than his usual work clothes, he had on a suit. This was the late 1970s, so it was a hideous pastel and polyester monstrosity, but it was a suit nonetheless. Three other men from his church got out of the car with him. Then another car pulled up, and out of it spilled four more men (all having been dressed at the same department store, apparently). These men began lugging brown paper sacks of groceries through our front door for what seemed like an hour. It wasn't Christmas. It wasn't Thanksgiving. It wasn't anyone's birthday. It was just on time.

Ironically, as Providence would have it, I had the honor of thanking a few of these men decades later by becoming their pastor, even delivering their eulogies. They had forgotten me, a curious, awkward, and Coke-bottle-glassed little boy who watched the parade of groceries enter my home so many years earlier. But I had not forgotten them—I never will—and I remain grateful for the simple kindness they showed to my family in our time of need. (And I'm thankful that in all those brown bags, there was not a single box of fish sticks!)

Those men didn't know it at the time, and I didn't either, but they did much more than deliver a few provisions to a needy family. They served Christ himself. No, no one in my family was magically or sacramentally transubstantiated into the living Lord, but Jesus was present that Saturday morning. He was more present than at any Communion table, more real than in any moment of prayer and more certain than in any flash of spiritual insight. He was there because my family was in need and that need was met by the love of others.

This final kingdom parable is Jesus' last public teaching before his Passion. It is, as it were, his final, compelling word, a word that could not be clearer: Jesus has identified with the weak and the marginalized in an unparalleled way. Yet, this has not prevented large segments of the church from attempting to evade his clear instructions. There are more than a dozen interpretations of this parable. They range far and wide over the theological field, but for simplification purposes, these can be reduced to two primary views (I resist making this type of generalization, but it would require multiple pages to catalog the various interpretations).

Those on the right, particularly those enamored by the apocalyptic nature of this parable, often apply incredible, elaborate interpretive schemes to the text, postponing its application until some millennial future. This allows the words of Jesus, with all its thorny implications, to be set aside. Those on the left have a different relationship with this parable. They love it and want to apply it wholesale to the world around us. Words and phrases like "social justice," "equality," and "equal opportunity" start getting thrown around (and these are very good words, mind you), as if the kingdom of God can be applied as a type of public policy. But I fear the right is a touch wrong and the left isn't quite right on this parable.

To those on the right I would say that while this parable is apocalyptic in nature, still it eliminates all speculation that the Good News of Jesus is purely spiritual or postponed to a later date. Final rewards are dispersed to the "goats" and the "sheep" based on the lives they lived in the here and now. So if the kingdom of God is anything at all, it is real, concrete, and practical today. There are people who are hungry right now, and their dying will not fix that. There are people suffering injustice today; ignoring them because "we'll understand it better by and by," is no excuse. There are people we encounter every day who are crushed by poverty, who are wrecked by addiction and enslavement, whose family life is a damnable disaster, who are so buried in debt, or who are so lonely and hopeless that the "one day after a while" offer of a heavenly condo is simply preposterous.

And to those on the left, while I applaud their zeal to better the lives of others, such zeal sometimes devolves into a sentimental, saccharin-sweet humanitarian effort to create a better world. Now, what's wrong with a better world? Nothing at all (just as there is nothing wrong with a condo in paradise)! But efforts at creating a more evenhanded society are not what the gospel or the kingdom is about! At the risk of being grossly misunderstood, Christians are not called to make the world a better place. They are called to live out the compassionate love of God. Granted, kindness toward those in need is not uniquely Christian. Followers of Jesus have not cornered the market on compassion, grace, and charity. But Christian compassion has a different source and impetus. It is not driven by an enlightened, magnanimous concern for our fellow human beings. It isn't concerned with humanity at all, not even those who suffer. Rather, our concern is driven by the kind of God we worship and the Jesus we follow.

I will state it clearly: this is neither a parable that explains a far-removed judgment nor one that "badgers people into loving one another."61 On the contrary, it reveals once again who Jesus really is. It reveals his profound love for the marginalized, the excluded, the feeble, and the hopeless; and he invites us to become participants in his love for others. Thus, our care and concern for others is not evidenced because of our own altruistic nature, but because our Lord identifies with and loves others, calling us to meet him there. "We love," as John says, "because he loved first" (1 John 4:19).

So this story says far more about God than it does about the world. It reveals more about who Jesus is than who we are. It shows us how to love more than how to act or what to believe. And it demonstrates God's immeasurable love, a love that stoops from heaven to the most remote corners of the world to identify with those who otherwise would have no identity at all. This change of perspective, that this is not a parable to be discounted or a sentiment to be artificially manufactured, empowers us to follow Jesus into the world animated by his love while discovering more and more of that love in those he called "the least of these."

Who are "the least?" Jesus makes it clear by repeating a list four different times in the parable. They are the hungry, the thirsty, the homeless, the naked (shivering), the sick, and the imprisoned. This list is reminiscent of Jesus' first public sermon, when he quoted the prophet Isaiah declaring that he had come to proclaim "Good News to the poor [the hungry, thirsty, homeless, and naked]. He has sent me to proclaim that captives will be released [the imprisoned], that the blind will see, that the oppressed will be set free [the sick], and that the time of the Lord's favor has come" (Luke 4:18–19). From the beginning of Jesus' ministry, to the very end of the age, Jesus is uniquely on the side of those who are weak, marginalized, and on the outside.

This startling revelation, that Jesus is "out there"—not figuratively, but literally—turns much of our preaching upside down (or right side up). We don't "take Jesus out to the world," as much as we meet him where he already is. Will Campbell, that old Mississippi Baptist "bootleg preacher," gave a sermon once critiquing the "invitation" as it is given in most of our revivalistic churches. He said, "Those of us who are acquainted with such invitations know that at the end of a sermon, the preacher invites people who want to commit their lives to Christ to come down the aisle to indicate that desire. I hope that someday there will be an evangelistic service in which, when the preacher gives the invitation and people start coming down the aisle, he yells back at them, 'Don't come down this aisle! Go to Jesus! Don't come to me! Go to Jesus!'"

He continues: "Upon that declaration, the people who were coming down the aisle turn around and exit the auditorium and get in their cars and drive away. He then yells at the rest of the congregation, 'Why are you hanging around here? Why don't you go to Jesus too? Why don't you all go to Jesus?' The people rise en masse and quickly leave the church, and soon the parking lot is empty. What I imagine is that about a half hour later the telephone at the police station starts ringing off the hook, and the voice at the other end says, 'We're down here at the old-folks home and there's some crazy people at the door yelling that they want to come in and visit Jesus, and I keep telling them Jesus isn't in here! All we have in here are a bunch of old ladies. But they keep saying, "But we want to visit Jesus! We want to visit Jesus!"'

"The next call is from the warden down at the prison. He's saying, 'Send some cops down here! There's a bunch of nuts at the gate and they're yelling and screaming, "Let us in there! We want to visit Jesus! We want to visit Jesus!" I keep telling them that all we have in this place are murderers, rapists, and thieves. But they keep yelling,

"Let us in! We want to visit Jesus!" No sooner does the cop hang up the phone than it rings again. This time it's the superintendent of the mental hospital calling for help. He's complaining that there are a bunch of weird people outside begging to be let in. They too want to see Jesus! The superintendent says, 'I keep telling them that Jesus isn't here. All we have here are a bunch of patients, but they keep yelling at us "We want to see Jesus!"62

Could it be more apparent? You will not find Jesus in heaven, reclining on a cloud. He isn't in church on Sunday morning, sitting in the pews. He isn't locked away in the Vatican or held hostage by a denominational seminary. Rather, Jesus is sitting in the emergency room, an uninsured, undocumented immigrant needing healing. He is behind bars, so far from his parole date he can't think that far into the future. He is homeless, evicted from his apartment, waiting in line at the shelter for a bed and a cup of soup. He is the poor child living in government housing with lice in his hair, the stripes of abuse on his body, and a growl in his stomach. He is an old forgotten woman in a roach-infested apartment who no one thinks of anymore. He is a refugee in Sudan, living in squalor. He is the abused and molested child who falsely feels responsible for the evil that is perpetrated against her. He is the young woman who hates herself for the decisions she has made, decisions that have imperiled her life, but did the best she could, torn between impossible choices. Jesus is anyone without power, ability, or the means to help themselves, and he beckons us to come to him, not on a do-gooding crusade, but in solidarity and embrace.

It is said that Saint Vincent de Paul, the great Catholic advocate for the poor, was once told about a poor beggar outside the church who needed help. Vincent finished serving the Eucharist to his congregation and said, "Then I am going *from* Jesus *to* Jesus." So literal was his understanding of this parabolic scene in Matthew 25, that he left the table of Christ's presence to find Christ's presence in "the least of these." And if any suspicion remains about Jesus' identification with such as these, we only need to remember that before this parable stopped echoing in his listeners' ears, Jesus became all of these things on his way to the cross: destitute, naked, imprisoned, friendless, and alone. His actions, as always, were consistent with his words.

It is this demand for consistency, with both words and actions, which may be the most forceful piece of this final story of Jesus. Eternal destinies, it seems, somehow hinge upon how we treat the weak. We can't simply call Jesus "Lord" and not be conduits of his compassion in the world. The "sheep" in this story, filled to overflowing kindness for the poor, are welcomed into the final kingdom with enthusiasm. The "goats," however, are turned away, their crime being a failure to love those who needed it. This is frightening scriptural ground upon which we "saved by grace alone" Protestants must navigate. Surely Jesus isn't saying that we can achieve salvation by just being kind to others, by working for it, is he? No, not quite.

Instead of seeing this parable as a *means* of obtaining salvation, it's better to read it as a *manifestation* of salvation. It's not a *door* to heaven; it is a *demonstration* of heaven come to earth. The "sheep" behave as they do, not because they think that they can get into the kingdom of God as a result (they were astounded at the King's final announcement, as they were not "keeping score"). They do as they do because the kingdom is already inside of them. The "sheep" scatter across the pastures of the world serving and loving others, not to earn their way into God's grace, but because the grace within them is already at work. In this regard, the parable has much in common with the famed "faith and deeds" passage of James 2.

The Apostle James, Jesus' brother and a leader in the early church, wrote one of the earliest communications to the fledgling Christian movement. At the end of chapter one and onward to chapter two of his letter, James challenged the early Christians to avoid discrimination, embrace mercy toward one another, and, suggestive of Jesus' own words, to graciously look after the marginalized (the widows and the orphans), which James considered the only "pure and faultless religion" (James 1:27). From there, James immediately launched into a bold discussion of "faith and deeds" and how they fit together. Faith, according to James, had to be much more than a spoken confession. Hell itself was capable of such intellectual assent. Rather, faith had to actually "work." There had to be good deeds attached to proper belief, or else the profession itself was dead. Faith had to actually make a difference in how we treated others.

So James and Jesus are speaking with the same voice. Neither of them claims that "deeds" lead to grace. "Deeds" flow out of the grace one has already received. True faith, the faith lived by the "sheep" in Jesus' parable, is proven by compassionate action. False faith, the faith professed by the "goats" in Jesus' parable, is likewise proven by the lack of compassionate action. The "goats" may have had orthodoxy on their side—that is, they professed rightly. But the "sheep" had orthopraxy on their side—they practiced rightly. This practice did not *produce* salvation; it was the *proof* that God's kingdom had come to rule in and over their hearts, resulting in loving service to others. Put plainly, dead faith says:

"Go in peace; keep warm and well fed," but does nothing about the physical needs of others.

It preaches how those who "don't work, shouldn't eat," but turns a blind eye to those who are starving because they are too old, too sick, or too weak to work.

It refuses to offer benevolence to the poor because God demands that we be "good stewards" of his money, as if God isn't in those who are rejected, literally asking for a little of his own money.

It rages against the evil of abortion but never opens its heart or home to teenage mothers or unwanted children.

It preaches the sanctity of traditional family values but will not defend the dignity or God-given value of others who are maligned because of their gender or sexuality.

It criticizes the crimes and chaos of the inner city, but quickly flees to the safety of the suburbs.

The "goats" always attempt to march to Zion all while leaving Jesus behind, for they never recognized him when he came to them.

A final story from Jewish historian Yaffa Eliach is fitting here, for it may be the most riveting modern representation of this parable, and it illustrates the revelatory nature of discovering Jesus in the most unexpected people. Yaffa, whose work ultimately found a home in the US Holocaust Museum, was born in Eišiškės, Lithuania, and she was a child when the Nazis overtook her village in 1941. An S.S. Death Squad accompanied the conquering army, and it went to work systematically massacring the Jews of the village. Victims were marched to a cemetery, forced to undress alongside a series of open trenches, and then shot. Their bodies spilt en masse into the graves. This disastrous scene was replayed over and over again, resulting in the deaths of more than three thousand Jewish men, women, and children.

One young man, sixteen-year-old Zvi Michalowski, happened to fall, very much alive, into the mass grave a nanosecond before the Nazi firing squad pulled their triggers. He waited beneath the dirt and the bodies of his friends and family until nightfall. Then, in the dark of night, Zvi struggled from the grave, cold, dirty, bloodied, and naked. At the far end of the cemetery he knew of some Christian families, and quickly he sought help from them. At house after house he was refused, left naked and afraid in the night. Finally he came to the home of a Christian widow who lived at the edge of the village near a forest.

When the old woman answered the door Zvi begged: "Please, let me come in." But the woman responded as all the others had, saying, "You belong in the cemetery, Jew!" Then, in a moment of desperate inspiration, Zvi replied, "But do you not recognize me? I am your Lord and Savior, Jesus Christ. I have come down from the cross to visit you. Look at my blood, my suffering, my innocence. Do not disown me." It was an epiphany. The old widow dropped to her knees weeping, kissing Zvi's blood-stained feet and crying out to God. Zvi remained safely with her for three days, and after convincing her to tell no one of his visit, he escaped to the forest supplied with the provisions he needed.63

- Did Jesus really visit the widow of Eišiškės on that evening? Yes, he did.

- Did the Messiah actually appear in a war-torn village in Lithuania? Absolutely.

- Did this surprise the old woman who received him into her home? Most assuredly.

- Did God crawl out of the grave seeking the help of someone who would care for him? Without a doubt, and he still does.

He will continue to appear and astonish us with his presence, a presence in the most unusual of circumstances and people. He reenters the world day after day in the "nobodies" of our society. He does so that we might find him anew, and in finding him, find the love that will save us and our world.

Conclusion

"God's kingdom is within you."

—LUKE 17:21 (CEV)

I SAT DOWN TO finish writing the conclusion for this book on a Friday afternoon. I had spent the morning busily locked away in my office and was oblivious to what was happening in the world at large. So before diving in to jot down these final words I took a break, poured a fresh cup of coffee, and turned on cable news. There on the screen were the dreadful images of Sandy Hook Elementary School. I was horror-struck, as was the entire nation, and this trivial little conclusion was set aside as I spent the rest of the day weeping in front of the television.

As the details of the tragedy began to emerge, I felt that nothing could be more appalling than what I was seeing and hearing. That was until several contemporary Christian leaders began commenting on the heartbreaking event. I realized that what I was seeing and hearing had indeed grown worse; for they began to explain the calamity of the innocent as God's wrath against the sins of others. It was malicious and cruel; and if there was a way to aggravate the suffering of these families further, these theological talking heads had accomplished exactly that.

Yet, I should not have been surprised, for it happens every time a disaster strikes. It doesn't matter if it is in Japan, Europe, Haiti, New Orleans, or Newtown. And it can be a tsunami, a hurricane, a theater shooting, or a house fire: pontificating preachers, televangelists, and their minions begin pointing fingers, blaming the victims, and speaking of God's raging vengeance against the world,

99

marking the "signs of the times." Even insurance companies, which usually stay out of theological matters, get in on the fault-finding. They refer to otherwise inexplicable natural tragedies as "acts of God." It seems that the only thing God is capable of, according to their attorneys and actuaries, is wrathful destruction.

Granted, I can't unravel the enigma that is a loving God presiding over an often unjust world, but I cannot accept the "act of God" explanation for so much misery—not in light of Jesus, and not in light of these beautiful, redemptive parables studied in the previous pages. This is why I'd like to redefine that phrase, "act of God," if I could. Instead of watching cable news for a cataclysmic disaster of the divine kind, or listening to the farcical explanations of today's prophets, or consulting your homeowners policy for the legalese, go look in the mirror. Indeed, you are an "act of God." You—the single, simple follower of Jesus—are God's gracious force of redemptive transformation in the world.

God does not cause suffering. Rather, it is God who enters the sorrow of this world and joins those victimized by it; he does that through you.

God is not lurking behind tragedy. Rather, he weeps with those left to bury their dead and put the pieces of their lives back together. This healing is accomplished through you.

God never systematically and vindictively plans disaster against the innocent. Rather, it is God who arrives in the recovering process for those who have faced injustice. This recovery shows up in and through you. You are an "act of God."

As a Christian, I believe that the greatest revelation the world has ever experienced is the appearance of Jesus Christ. I believe that he was truly God in the flesh. There have been plenty of divine representatives throughout world and religious history, but only in Jesus is there this principle of incarnation: the divine really inhabited a human body. This is an astounding confession of faith, but if it is true as Christians believe, one only needs to look as far as Jesus to know God. This is the best of good news, for we understand that God has gladly come to us on an earth-shaking and redeeming mission, a mission that Jesus called the kingdom of God.

But here is something even more astounding: the Christ sent from God as God, now sends us into the world to do his work and bear his image. While there was only one unique incarnation of God in the flesh, there is a genuine ongoing extension of that incarnation in every person who submits his or her will to the way of Jesus. Thus, you are an "act of God," an authorized, empowered, commissioned ambassador of heaven sent to embody his redemption and grace on earth.

"I am sending you," Jesus said, "just as the Father has sent me." (John 20:21 CEV). Or as Jesus would also say, "God's kingdom is within you" (Luke 17:21 CEV), and that kingdom is just itching to be set free in the world.

Such words always remind me of my friend Walt DeNero. Until his retirement Walt was the director of the University of Georgia's Fanning Leadership Center. He was one of the finest public servants I ever met, and after almost going into the priesthood as a young man, he decided instead he wanted a family. So he used all his holy energy and focused his calling on public life, and did so with unparalleled grace and expertise.

Whenever he would give a talk (and these talks were always delivered with the passion of a homily rather than the sterility of a lecture), he would conclude his talk with the same story—always the same story—because more than anything, Walt wanted people to enter the world in service to others.

The story is about two log-sitting turtles who were discussing world events. One turtle said, "I wonder why God allows so much suffering in the world? Why is there so much hunger, so much war, so much sickness, and so much heartache? Sometimes I'd like to ask him 'Why?' when he could do something about it." After a little while the other turtle said, "Well, why don't you ask God that question?" And the first one responded, "No. I won't ask that question. I am afraid God might ask me the same thing."

I have heard Walt tell that story on a dozen different occasions. After his fifth or sixth recitation, I thought, "I wish Walt would get some new material," but after hearing the story so often, I actually began to get it. Maybe that's why he tells it over and over. It takes us all a while to understand.

This is what I have come to understand: the day will come—and I believe this with all of my heart—when the world will have no more injustice, no more evil, no more fear, no more hate, violence, or sin. There will be no more maimed and bullet-ridden soldiers; no more hungry children; no more school shootings; no more battered wives; no more drug addictions; no more refugees, homelessness, poverty, or abuse. I also understand—and I believe this too with all of my heart—that I cannot simply wait for that world to magically arrive.

If I believe that one day the lamb will lay down with the lion, that swords will be beaten into plowshares, that mercy and justice will flow down like the waters, that every tear will be wiped away from our eyes, and there will be no more death or sorrow or crying or pain, then I can't loiter about earth ignoring the heaven that demands to come to fruition today. I have to believe it now, and I have to live it now. I have to act out the kingdom of God in this very moment because God might ask of me what I would ask of him: "Why won't you do something about this world, when it is within your power to do so?"

Living out the kingdom of God requires that I—we—become active participants, "acts of God," in the redemptive process. We participate in the kingdom of God, recognizing that God has intertwined his kingdom with his people, and when we join that kingdom, we become what God wants for his world: the reality and expression of the redeeming Jesus.

God has the power of heaven, and we have a presence here on earth. Put together, this is how God's kingdom comes. Or as Desmond Tutu put it so eloquently, "Without God, we cannot; but without us, God will not. Such is the kingdom of heaven."64

May that kingdom come—it's not that far away—and may it begin in you and in me.

Endnotes

1. Based on Frost, "A Trip to Paradise," Archive 2004.
2. Thoreau, *Walden*, 217.
3. McBrayer, *Leaving Religion, Following Jesus*, 8–9.
4. "Widgetized" is a word I use to describe the prevailing approach to spiritual formation today, whereby the gospel is reduced to easy accessible explanations and applications. On the contrary, Jesus never explained the kingdom of God, he only described it.
5. The late Clarence Jordan always defined the kingdom of God as the "God Movement."
6. Il-Sung, *With the Century*, 62–63.
7. Marx, *Critique of Hegel's Philosophy of Right*, 4.
8. McBrayer, *A Christmas Vigil*, unit 3.
9. Edwards, "Sinners in the Hands of an Angry God," 404–18.
10. Leonard, "An Audacious Identity."
11. Edwards, 404–18.
12. Zurheide, "Herschel Hobbs on Baptist Freedom."
13. Haselmayer, et al., *A Is for Abductive*, 115.
14. Steinbeck, *The Pearl*, 65.
15. Lenski, *Power and Privilege*, 215–81.
16. Ibid., 281.
17. Weil, *Gravity and Grace*, 10.
18. Tolstoy, *The Kingdom of God Is Within You*, 31.
19. Weil, 10.
20. Matthews, "Zell Miller's Hardball Interview."
21. Gladwell, "Harlan, Kentucky: 'Die Like a Man, Like Your Brother Did,'" 161–76.
22. Ibid., 169.
23. Muller, *How Then, Shall We Live*, 99.
24. McBrayer, "Life in the Mailroom."
25. Based on Manning, *The Ragamuffin Gospel*, 53.
26. Barth, *Church Dogmatics*, 4.3.2.
27. Gorres, *The Hidden Face*, 331.
28. Martin, *Autobiography*, 113.
29. Dalrymple, *Nine Lives*, 141.
30. Hawthorne, *The Scarlet Letter*, 175.
31. Witherington, *Matthew*, 353.

32. Stewart, *Jacobellis v. Ohio.*
33. Ten Boom, *The Hiding Place.*
34. Ten Boom, *Tramp for the Lord*, 53–56.
35. Based on Patton, *Pastoral Care in Context*, 181.
36. Mohney, "Man Reported to Find $500,000 Worth of Treasure in Storage Unit."
37. Luskin, "The Necessity of Forgiveness."
38. For more information about Amy Biehl visit http://www.amybiehl. co.za/.
39. Lewis, *The Great Divorce.*
40. Ibid., 25–31.
41. King, "I Have a Dream."
42. Ibid.
43. McBrayer, *Leaving Religion, Following Jesus*, 97.
44. Based on DeChant and Fasching, *Comparative Religious Ethics*, 16–20.
45. My reference may be an exaggeration, but the scene of Ralph's rescue upon the arrival of the Royal Navy came immediately to mind. See Golding, "Cry of the Hunters," *Lord of the Flies*, 259–85.
46. For more on this "us versus them" entrenchment, see McLaren, *Why Did Jesus, Moses, the Buddha, and Mohammed Cross the Road*, 40–53.
47. Wells, *War of the Worlds.*
48. Welles, et al, *War of the Worlds*, CD.
49. Jenkins and LaHaye, *Left Behind.*
50. To see more visit www.leftbehind.com.
51. Bliss, *Memoirs of William Miller*, 79.
52. Brand, "The Clock and Library Projects."
53. Ibid.
54. Claiborne, "Keynote Address."
55. Crossan, *The Historical Jesus*, 99, 221.
56. For more on this alternative interpretation, and others, see Herzog's *Subversive Speech.*
57. Yoder, *The Politics of Jesus*, 154.
58. Romero, *Voice of the Voiceless*, 177–87.
59. Romero, "The Last Sermon."
60. Zagano, *Twentieth-Century Apostles*, 119.
61. Goode, *Crashing the Idols*, 116.
62. Campolo, *Let Me Tell You a Story*, 30–31.
63. Michalowski survived the Holocaust. This telling of his story is based on Eliach, *Hasidic Tales of the Holocaust*, 53–55.
64. As quoted by Crossan, "Will the Real Jesus Please Rise," audio.

Bibliography

Barth, Karl. *Church Dogmatics.* Edinburgh: Clark, 1961. 4.3.2.

Bliss, Sylvester. *Memoirs of William Miller.* Boston: Joshua V. Himes, 1853.

Brand, Stewart. "The Clock and Library Projects." No pages. Online: http://longnow.org/about/.

Campolo, Tony. *Let Me Tell You a Story.* Nashville: W Publishing, 2000.

Claiborne, Shane. "Keynote Address." Speech at the Clarence Jordan Symposium, Americus, GA, September 29, 2012.

Crossan, John Dominic. *The Historical Jesus.* New York: HarperCollins, 1992.

————. "Will the Real Jesus Please Rise." Interview by John Shuck, June 7, 2012. No pages. Online: http://progressivechristianity.org/events/john-dominic-crossan-interviewed-by-john-shuck/.

Dalrymple, William. *Nine Lives: In Search of the Sacred in Modern India.* New York: Vintage, 2011.

DeChant, Dell, and Darrell J. Fasching. *Comparative Religious Ethics: A Narrative Approach.* Reprint. Malden, MA: Blackwell, 2004.

Edwards, Jonathan. "Sinners in the Hands of an Angry God." In *The Works of Jonathan Edwards, Volume 22, Sermons and Discourses, 1739–1742,* edited by Harry S. Trout et al., 404–418. New Haven: Yale University Press, 2003.

Eliach, Yaffa. *Hasidic Tales of the Holocaust.* New York: Vintage, 1988.

Frost, Peter. "A Trip to Paradise." *The Jewish Magazine,* Issue Number 83 (September–October 2004). No pages. Online: http://jewishmag.com/83mag/chelm/chelm.htm.

Gladwell, Malcolm. "Harlan, Kentucky: 'Die Like a Man, Like Your Brother Did.'" In *Outliers: The Story of Success.* New York: Hachette, 2008.

Golding, William. "Cry of the Hunters." In *Lord of the Flies.* New York: Perigee, 2011.

Goode, Richard C. *Crashing the Idols: The Vocation of Will D. Campbell (and Any Other Christian for That Matter).* Eugene: Cascade, 2010.

Gorres, Ida Friederike. *The Hidden Face.* San Francisco: Ignatius, 1959.

Haselmayer, Jerry, et al. *A Is for Abductive: The Language of the Emerging Church.* Grand Rapids: Zondervan, 2003.

Hawthorne, Nathaniel. *The Scarlet Letter.* Mineola: Dover, 1994.

Herzog II, William R. *Subversive Speech: Jesus as Pedagogue of the Oppressed.* Louisville: Westminster John Knox, 1994.

Bibliography

Il-Sung, Kim. *With the Century.* Pyongyang, North Korea: Korean Friendship Association (2003) 62–63. Online http://www.korea-dpr.com/lib/202.pdf.

Jenkins, Jerry B. and Tim LaHaye. *Left Behind: A Novel of the Earth's Last Days.* Carol Stream: Tyndale, 1995.

King Jr., Martin Luther. "I Have a Dream." Speech, Washington, D.C., August 27, 1963.

Lenski, Gerhard E. *Power and Privilege: A Theory of Social Stratification.* New York: McGraw Hill, 1966.

Leonard, Bill. "An Audacious Identity." Sermon, Charlotte, NC, June 24, 2010.

Lewis, C.S. *The Great Divorce.* New York: HarperCollins, 2001.

Luskin, Fred. "The Necessity of Forgiveness." No pages. Online: http://www.pbs.org/kqed/onenight/stories/forgive/index.html.

Manning, Brennan. *The Ragamuffin Gospel: Good News for the Bedraggled, Beat-Up, and Burnt Out.* Colorado Springs: Multnomah, 2005.

Martin, Thérèse. *The Autobiography of Saint Thérèse of Lisieux: The Story of a Soul.* Translated by John Beevers. NewYork: Double Day, 2001.

Marx, Karl. *Critique of Hegel's Philosophy of Right.* Chicago: Aristeus, 2012.

Matthews, Chris. "Zell Miller's Hardball Interview." No pages. Online: http://www.msnbc.msn.com/id/7644466/ns/msnbc-hardball_with_chris_matthews/t/zell-millers-hardball-interview/#.ULVPF4fAeSo

McBrayer, Ronnie. *A Christmas Vigil.* Macon: Smyth and Helwys, 2010.

———. *Leaving Religion, Following Jesus.* Macon: Smyth and Helwys, 2009.

———. "Life in the Mailroom." No pages. Online: http://blog.nola.com/cest-la-nola/2012/04/life_in_the_mailroom.html

McLaren, Brian. *Why Did Jesus, Moses, the Buddha, and Mohammed Cross the Road?* New York: Jericho, 2012.

Mohney, Gillian. "Man Reported to Find $500,000 Worth of Treasure in Storage Unit." No pages. Online: http://abcnews.go.com/US/man-reported-find-500000-worth-treasure-storage-unit/story?id=14958206#.T1qlfzEgffs.

Muller, Wayne. *How Then, Shall We Live: Four Simple Questions That Reveal the Beauty and Meaning of Our Lives.* New York: Bantam, 2007.

Patton, John. *Pastoral Care in Context.* Louisville: Westminster John Knox, 2005.

Romero, Oscar. "The Last Sermon; March 23, 1980." No pages. Online: http://www.haverford.edu/relg/faculty/amcguire/romero.html.

———. *Voice of the Voiceless: The Four Pastoral Letters and Other Statements.* Maryknoll, NY: Orbis, 177–87.

Steinbeck, John. *The Pearl.* New York: Penguin, 2002.

Ten Boom, Corrie. *The Hiding Place.* New York: Bantam, 1974.

———. *Tramp for the Lord.* New York: Jove, 1978.

Thoreau, David Henry. *Walden.* New York: Empire, 2012.

Tolstoy, Leo. *The Kingdom of God Is Within You.* Seattle: Pacific, 2010.

Weil, Simone. *Gravity and Grace.* New York: Routledge, 2002.

Welles, Orson. *War of the Worlds; Original 1938 Radio Broadcast.* Audio CD. Buckinghamshire: Pickwick, 2006.

Wells, H.G. *War of the Worlds*. Portsmouth, NH: Heinemann, 1951.

Witherington III, Ben. *Matthew*. Macon: Smyth and Helwys, 2006.

Yoder, John Howard. *The Politics of Jesus*. Second Edition. Grand Rapids: Eerdmans, 1994.

Zagano, Phyllis. *Twentieth-Century Apostles: Contemporary Spirituality in Action*. Collegeville, MN: Liturgical, 1999.

Zurheide, Jeffry. "Herschel Hobbs on Baptist Freedom." Lecture, Shawnee, OK, November 29, 2000.

Lightning Source UK Ltd.
Milton Keynes UK
UKOW01f1219050218

317386UK00007B/845/P